☀ THE ☀
Fair Trade

INGREDIENT

::: COOKBOOK :::

THE Fair Trade INGREDIENT COOKBOOK

NETTIE CRONISH

whitecap

EDITOR Penny Hozy
PROOFREADER Patrick Geraghty
DESIGN Andrew Bagatella
PHOTOGRAPHY BY Mike McColl (recipe and ingredients photos). Éric St. Pierre
(farm photos).

Library and Archives Canada Cataloguing in Publication

Title: The fair trade ingredient cookbook/Nettie Cronish.
Names: Cronish, Nettie, 1954- author.
Description: Includes index.
Identifiers: Canadiana 20210094672 | ISBN 9781770503304 (softcover)
Subjects: LCSH: Cooking. | LCSH: Fair trade foods. | LCGFT: Cookbooks.
Classification: LCC TX714 .C76 2021 | DDC 641.5—dc23

We acknowledge the financial support of the Government of Canada through the Canada
Book Fund (CBF) for our publishing activities and the Province of British Columbia through the
Book Publishing Tax Credit.

Nous reconnaissons l'appui financier du gouvernement du Canada et la province de la Colom-
bie-Britannique par le Book Publishing Tax Credit.

Printed in Hong Kong

7 6 5 4 3 2 1

To the memory of Lyell W. M. Cook, fair trade advocate and enthusiast.

CONTENTS

FOREWORD

A Message from John Kay
Former Chair of Fairtrade Canada

Food is a universal language. It defines us. It brings us together. It tells our stories. Food takes us on a journey of discovery and delight. Food reveals and celebrates our common humanity.

Fair trade is also a global language. A global language of shared community. A global language of hope for a just and fair world for all. Fair trade brings together the cocoa farmers of Ghana with the spice growers of Sri Lanka; the campesino coffee growers of Chiapas with the banana farmers and workers of Ecuador. Fair trade is the story of farmers and workers in the Global South, of coffee roasters and chocolate lovers in North America, sharing the global language of hope for a better world.

In 2003, I first met Nettie Cronish when she joined the Board of Fairtrade Canada. During our 10-year journey together on the Board, Nettie and I were privileged to work with our board and staff colleagues—and with the entire global fair trade movement—to share fair trade's story. We told the story of a global community sharing and celebrating the promise of a more just world. A world rooted in the global language of food.

The language of fair trade is the language of small-holder coffee farmers building their communities and their livelihoods free of exploitation. It is the story of chocolate—our sweetest food delight—produced without the scourge of child labor. Fairtrade is the story of farmers in the Global South being paid fairly for the abundant and joyous fruits of their labor.

The recipes in this book explore the languages of food and fair trade. When you prepare these recipes—whether alone or in the company of family and friends—I hope you will celebrate and enjoy the story they tell of our shared global humanity.

FAIRTRADE CERTIFICATION

"Fair trade" is a general term describing trading relationships based on fairness, transparency, and respect. It is a different way of doing business that aims to ensure that farmers and workers in developing countries get a fair deal. Consumers are being bombarded with many ethical business claims. It is my belief that Fairtrade and Fair for Life are the two best certifiers when it comes to environmental concerns, ethical business practices, workplace standards, and supply chain management. They offer the most transparent, sustainable business models.

In this cookbook I will be dealing with two fair trade certification designations: Fairtrade and Fair for Life. They each have their own page explaining their history and certification practices.

I wanted to write this cookbook because it is important to understand what fair trade is about and how one can live a "fair trade life." As a past member of the Fairtrade Canada board, I have met many producers, farmers, and businesspeople, and I know that fair trade certification contributes to sustainability and ethical decisions. Many people through their place of worship promote fair trade (see Harry Cook's fair trade coffee initiative, page 11), and colleges and universities introduce students to fair trade coffee, tea, and sugar and prove that profit and principle can co-exist. As students begin their independent life (and find a job) they will continue to buy fair trade products.

Official Fairtrade certification provides an independent third party assurance that a product meets internationally recognized fair trade standards. With so many labels proclaiming "fair trade" at stores, it's hard to know which ones to buy. Anyone can use the terms "fair trade" or "fairly traded." Fairtrade-certified products will carry the Fairtrade certification mark.

You see it on labels for bananas, coconut, chocolate, cocoa, coffee, flowers, olive oil, quinoa, rice, spices, and tea that are used in this book. "Fairtrade" assists consumers in supporting products that come from producer co-ops that have been certified and are audited to ensure compliance with Fairtrade standards. Producers are paid a guaranteed base price that covers the cost of production plus the Fairtrade Premium, an additional sum that the cooperatives democratically choose to invest in what their community requires most, such as healthcare initiatives, education, women's leadership programs, and training.

Fairtrade also supports producers to become more climate resilient through environmental standards, empowering farmers to pursue organic farming, shade-grown coffee, reforestation projects, water conservation programs, and environmentally friendly practices.

FAIRTRADE CANADA

In 1988, the first fair trade label, Max Havelaar, was established. The launch of the Max Havelaar label was an important development in the fair trade movement because it introduced certified products to consumers in a significant and meaningful way. While fair trade products existed before, they were only sold in small specialty shops. Max Havelaar introduced fair trade to mainstream consumers through supermarkets.

Since its inception, the international Fairtrade label has grown to represent the world's largest and most recognized fair trade system. Currently, Fairtrade includes three producer networks, 25 national fair trade organizations, Fairtrade International, and FLOCERT, the independent certification body of the global Fairtrade system. Each plays a unique role in achieving Fairtrade's vision and delivering impacts for farmers and workers.

Fairtrade Canada was founded in 1994 as a volunteer-based organization. Today, it is a national, nonprofit fair trade licensing and public education organization.

EDUCATION

Fairtrade Canada works alongside community groups, companies, and individual citizens to educate about fair trade and Fairtrade-certified products. Through partnerships, campaigns, promotional materials, events, and media engagement, Fairtrade Canada helps Canadians understand the importance of trade justice so more producers can sell more of their products on fair terms.

WHAT FAIRTRADE STANDS FOR

Fairtrade standards are known for their rigor and highly credible development process. Fairtrade regularly consults stakeholders—including farmers, traders, businesses, and NGOs—to evaluate and update our standards in an open and transparent process. The Fairtrade system is 50% owned and governed by producers, who have an equal say in any decisions.

®

FAIRTRADE

info.fairtrade.net

Key components of Fairtrade's standards are:

- **Fairtrade minimum price** (a guaranteed base price that covers the producers' cost of production, which protects producers when market prices fall)
- **Fairtrade Premium** (additional funds for producers to invest in community or business development projects)
- **Democratic decision-making by producers**
- **Long-term, dependable contracts with buyers**
- **Sustainable environmental practices**
- **Adherence to core International Labour Organization conventions**

Fairtrade Canada is a national, nonprofit Fairtrade licensing and public education organization, and the only Canadian member of Fairtrade International (FLO).

Currently, Fairtrade Canada has 150 licensees who sell fair trade products. They are based in Ottawa, Ontario.

WHY YOU SHOULD BUY FAIR TRADE PRODUCTS

We live in an age when consumers are more informed than ever about what they buy, eat, and use. Local producers and chefs are informing their customers where the food they consume comes from and how it was grown or raised. People are eager to educate themselves and spend money on products and ingredients that benefit their bodies, environment, and communities. That is why buying fair trade ingredients has a tremendous social impact. They have an ethical integrity.

In this cookbook, I want to give the consumer an understanding of the process, explaining how an ingredient qualifies for Fairtrade certification and detail the steps involved in how that product reaches a supermarket shelf. Some chapters will have an interview with a fair trade producer co-operative that will provide background information, describe the benefits of belonging to the Fairtrade certification program, and outline their business model. Awareness of Fairtrade certification means most global coffee shops offer fair trade coffee on their menus, while shoppers can buy bananas, chocolate, cocoa powder, coconut milk, coffee, olive oil, quinoa, spices, sugar, tea, vanilla, and so much more in major supermarkets. Shopping ethically really does change lives and communities for the better.

The book has 94 recipes, all professionally tested. As a past member of the Fairtrade Canada board and as a vegetarian/vegan/flexitarian chef, I want to reach as many people as possible. I teach cooking classes at major

Canadian supermarkets. Through my classes, I have an opportunity to introduce, promote, and educate consumers about the use of fair trade ingredients in their pantries. This cookbook will provide delicious, easy-to-prepare recipes using the ingredients that have been profiled, and trace their origins back to fair trade producers.

FAIR FOR LIFE CERTIFICATION

Fair for Life is a fair trade certification program for food, cosmetic, textile, and handicraft products derived through responsible supply chains.

HISTORY

In the early 2000s, there were limited certification options for companies and organizations wishing to attest to the fair trade nature of their commercial partnerships. The Fair for Life label was developed in 2006 to create an opportunity for previously excluded products and authentic fair trade producers and buyers to be eligible to participate in fair trade certifications, under a new approach. Fair for Life is currently managed by the ECOCERT Group, headquartered in France.

The ECOCERT Group is a certification body for sustainable development and currently the international leader for organic certifications. With 30 subsidiaries in 26 countries, ECOCERT operates in more than 130 countries, offering various social and environmental certifications and training, consulting, and privacy standards. The Fair for Life program has a regional hub in the Canadian office, based in Quebec City, Quebec, that is responsible for North American certifications.

Fair for Life has evolved over the years into a rigorous certification with over 350 operations, producing over 3,500 certified products in nearly 50 countries. The program draws strength from an international network of auditors with local knowledge and languages, allowing for a standard with strict social and environmental criteria, while remaining adaptable to local contexts.

The Fair for Life label integrates the international principals of Fairtrade, International Labor Organization conventions, SA8000 criteria for worker rights, and social criteria of the International Federation of Organic Agriculture Movements (IFOAM). The program guarantees that human rights are protected at key stages of the supply chain and that the producers and workers around the world benefit from good working conditions and a fair remuneration verified through an independent and impartial third party.

Fair for Life adopts an approach of empowerment and accountability of certified operations by recognizing that companies and organizations are the changemakers. By facilitating, framing, and verifying their progress and commitments on fair trade, Fair for Life provides a structure and guarantee that is quite unlike any other fair trade certification.

For more info, see www.fairforlife.org.

Krista Pineau
North American Coordinator and Certification Officer, Fair for Life

PARISH OF FRENCH VILLAGE FAIR TRADE COFFEE INITIATIVE

As a business consultant, I was engaged by Just Us Coffee Roasters to complete a business plan at their office located in Grand Pre, Nova Scotia, an hour's drive west of Halifax. Just Us was the first Fairtrade coffee roaster in Canada. The business was started by Debbie and Jeff Moore, who mortgaged their home to buy their first container of coffee beans, and learned how to roast the beans on their own. I had never heard of Fairtrade prior to working with Just Us, but became fascinated with the concept over the course of completing my project there.

When I finished the business plan, I asked Jeff Moore, the founder of Just Us, "If someone wanted to get involved in Fairtrade, how would they go about it?" He placed a call to the Executive Director of Fairtrade Canada, located in Ottawa, Ontario, who told him that they happened to be looking for someone to add to their board. She came to Nova Scotia to interview me and I ended up on the board as Treasurer for the next 10 years. I was the first professional accountant to have been appointed to their board, and the first to have taken on the position of Treasurer. Nettie Cronish and I both joined the board of directors of Fairtrade Canada that same year. We became good friends and have remained so ever since.

At the time, I was the Warden of the Anglican Parish of French Village here in Nova Scotia, which is made up of four churches located in four small communities surrounding St. Margaret's Bay. There are approximately 250 families that make up the congregation of the Parish. Like most churches at that time, the individual churches in the Parish were having financial difficulties and needed to stimulate growth among the congregations. I put two and two together and realized that, although there would be no direct financial benefit to the Parish from a fair trade initiative, it might just be the vehicle to help stimulate growth in the congregation through a common objective that the congregation could get behind.

This initiative started in 2006 as an outreach project of the Anglican Parish of French Village, located 30 kilometers south of Halifax. It has expanded over the years to include supporters who were not aligned with the Parish but who supported the initiative in an effort to support fair trade coffee growers in Mexico.

As a group of volunteers, we sold fair trade coffee on a subscription basis where we delivered a bag of coffee or tea to the participants every month until they told us to stop. One hundred percent of the profits from this initiative went back to the coffee growers in Mexico who worked so hard to produce the coffee we enjoyed here in Canada.

The initiative supported some of the needs of the hard-working coffee growers and their families in a small village high in the mountains of southern Mexico called Buena Vista, Oaxaca State, Mexico. It was an initiative where one small community in Nova Scotia was helping another small community in Mexico.

The fair trade movement provides the fair trade coffee growers with an alternate market into which they can sell their coffee, which in turn allows the participating members to pay a fair wage to the hard-working people who grow the coffee, plus it helps provide money for clinics, clean water, schools, etc. . . . it is not charity. It is paying people a fair wage for their labor so they can feed themselves and their families and, with the Fairtrade Premium, provide the basic necessities of life as well as an opportunity for an education. The Fairtrade Premium is the additional money built into the price charged for Fairtrade coffee that is collected by the coffee co-ops. This Premium is used to build infrastructure to benefit the producers and their families.

My contact in Buena Vista was Father Francisco van der Hoff, a Dutch worker priest and the founder of the Fairtrade coffee label in the early 1980s, who I had met through Just Us when he came to Nova Scotia to visit Jeff Moore. You can find information on Father van der Hoff at http://en.wikipedia.org/wiki/Frans_van_der_Hoff.

Fr. van der Hoff was gracious enough to have visited the Parish several years ago and participated in the service with Fr. Mark, and most recently agreed to attend a service at St. Georges Church on June 9, 2013, with Rev. Brieanna.

In the 12 years that this initiative has been reaching out to the people of Buena Vista, it has:

1. **Purchased a satellite dish, computer and training** so the people in the village can access the internet and communicate using Skype, at no cost, to the next village or around the world.
2. **Purchased a community generator** because they are so far up the mountain that if a storm blows down a power pole, they must wait days or weeks before electricity is restored.
3. **Built a kindergarten** for the young children in the village.
4. **Purchased eight streetlights** for the village because, prior to this, there was no light and the streets are rough and dangerous to travel

at night. Also, in year four we had an extra $1,000 accumulated at the time of the earthquake in Haiti. When asked, the supporters of the initiative unanimously agreed to donate the surplus $1,000 to help with relief efforts.

5. **Committed to sponsoring three young women** who graduated from high school in the village and expressed a desire to go on to university. A university degree will not only lift these young women out of the cycle of poverty, it will also lift their families out of poverty.

6. **Funded a "pilot project" designed to provide mobile medical care** to people in remote villages based on a model originating in Cuba. If the project is evaluated and deemed viable, the Mexican government has agreed to fund it on a permanent basis. In year six we also supported the building of an **aquaculture project** in the village, large enough to raise 4,000 freshwater fish called Tilapia per year, providing the villagers with an additional source of protein as well as some additional income.

7. **Upgraded U.C.I.R.I.'s (the workers' co-op) communication equipment** ($2,000) and **sponsored three poultry projects** ($3,000) to be run by youth in the villages.

8. **Established new coffee plants** after a rust from Central America wiped out 70% of the coffee plants.

9. **Built greenhouses to diversify the economy** as a partial alternative to 100% dependence on coffee.

10. **Repaired greenhouses** in Buena Vista after a hurricane.

11. **Raised $30,000** for earthquake relief after Oaxaca was hit with two large earthquakes.

12. **Provided additional help with earthquake recovery.**

Harry Cook
Fair Trade Initiative Coordinator

FAIR TRADE
PRODUCER LOCATIONS

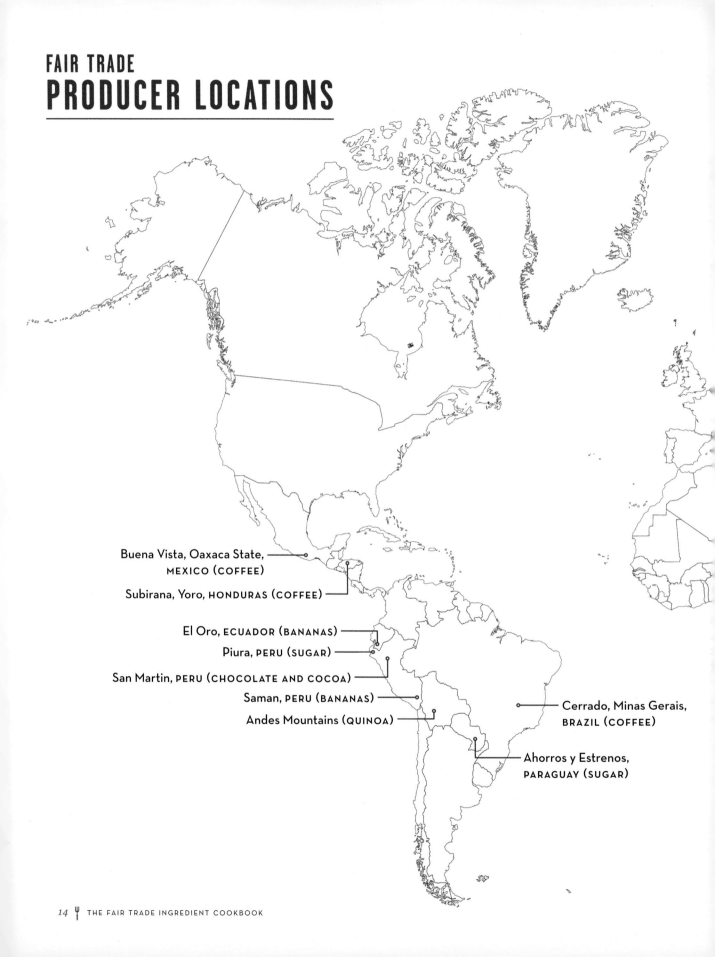

Buena Vista, Oaxaca State, MEXICO (COFFEE)

Subirana, Yoro, HONDURAS (COFFEE)

El Oro, ECUADOR (BANANAS)

Piura, PERU (SUGAR)

San Martin, PERU (CHOCOLATE AND COCOA)

Saman, PERU (BANANAS)

Andes Mountains (QUINOA)

Cerrado, Minas Gerais, BRAZIL (COFFEE)

Ahorros y Estrenos, PARAGUAY (SUGAR)

Burqin
and Jenin,
PALESTINE
(OLIVE OIL)

Matale,
Central Province,
SRI LANKA
(COCONUT MILK)

Chapter One

FAIR TRADE
BANANAS

FAIR TRADE
BANANAS

Equifruit

Established in 2006, Equifruit is Canada's leading Fairtrade-certified banana importer and marketer. They insist on being "Fair from the Start" and advocate greatly for the rights of small producers and plantation workers to ensure a fair distribution of value along the banana supply chain. They work with a network of retailers and distributors in Ontario and Quebec.

Fairtrade certification allows farmers to be paid a living wage, ensures safe working conditions, and emphasizes sustainable agricultural practices. Buyers agree to respect Fairtrade minimum prices, which represent the cost of sustainable production, and contribute an additional amount, called the Fairtrade Social Premium, which is used by producers and workers to invest in community development projects. In the case of bananas, the Fairtrade Premium is set at 1 USD per 40-lb case.

Equifruit has developed close relationships with their grower partners APPBOSA and Asoguabo. APPBOSA (ah-peh-peh-boss-ah) is a co-op consisting of 555 small producers, who started exporting Fairtrade bananas in 2003. Collectively, they farm about 600 hectares in northwest Peru and employ 385 community members. Being able to decide how Fairtrade premiums are spent gives producers the ability to decide what is best for their businesses and communities, including investments in quality local health centers, schools, and portable running water in their homes, to name just a few projects. To make their farms more efficient, APPBOSA invested premiums into the construction of a cable system to allow the easy transportation of bananas from the farm to packing stations with less back-breaking labor.

Asoguabo (ah-sew-gwah-boh) is a cooperative located in the El Oro province in southwestern Ecuador. Founded by 14 small scale farmers in 1998, they pooled their efforts to sell directly to the export market, thus bypassing the need for a middleman to sell to the big banana companies. Today, they have grown to be one of the largest fair trade banana exporters

in Ecuador, with 132 small-holder banana farms. School supplies, retirement care, and safe drinking water are just a few benefits from their investments in the community through the Fairtrade Social Premium. Being able to engage with sustainable initiatives on their farms allows for better working conditions and agricultural practices. Asoguabo's fair treatment of workers and sustainable organic farming is often used as a national benchmark by Ecuador's Ministry of Agriculture.

For more info, see www.equifruit.com.

BANANA CHIP BROWNIES

MAKES 10 BROWNIES

1 cup (250 mL) dark
brown sugar

2 large eggs

½ cup (120 mL) olive oil

½ cup (120 mL) coconut milk

1 tsp (5 mL) vanilla extract

¾ cup (180 mL) unbleached
white flour

⅓ cup (80 mL) cocoa powder

1 tbsp (15 mL) arrowroot flour

½ tsp (2 mL) sea salt

¼ tsp (1 mL) baking powder

½ cup (120 mL) dried banana
chips, chopped

½ cup (120 mL) mini
chocolate chips

⅓ cup (80 mL) walnuts,
coarsely chopped

3 tbsp (45 mL) unsweetened
shredded coconut

These brownies are very chewy. I like to scatter the dried banana pieces with the chocolate chips over the mixture before baking and gently press down with a large fork. The surface remains moist and each bite is sweet and tasty.

1. Preheat oven to 350°F (180°C). Lightly oil a 9-inch (23 cm) square pan and set aside.

2. In a medium-size bowl, stir together the sugar, eggs, oil, milk, and vanilla. Whisk to combine.

3. In a small bowl, add the flour, cocoa powder, arrowroot flour, salt, and baking powder. Stir well to combine.

4. Add the dry ingredients to the wet ingredients. Stir to combine. Pour the batter into the prepared pan. Evenly scatter the banana chips, chocolate chips, walnuts, and coconut over top, and press down gently with a fork.

5. Bake for 35 minutes or until set in the center. Allow to cool before cutting into pieces.

BANANA PINEAPPLE CHERRY COOKIES

MAKES 3 DOZEN

Combining fresh and dried fruit is a great way to ensure your baked goods are not overly sweet. Banana and pineapple pair so well, you can almost feel a tropical breeze.

....

1. Heat oven to 375°F (190°C). Line 2 rimmed baking sheets with parchment paper.

2. In a medium-size bowl, combine the flour, baking powder, baking soda, salt, and cardamom.

3. Using a stand mixer, beat the butter, sugar, and banana on medium speed until creamy. Add the egg and vanilla. Mix until combined.

4. On low speed, beat in the flour mixture. Stir in the chocolate chips, cherries, coconut, pineapple, and macadamia nuts.

5. Drop by rounded tablespoonfuls onto the baking sheets, spacing 2 inches (5 cm) apart.

6. Bake in the oven for 10 to 15 minutes, or until bottoms are golden. Cool cookies on baking sheets on wire racks for 5 minutes. Remove from pan to rack; let cool completely.

1⅔ cups (400 mL) unbleached white flour

¾ tsp (4 mL) baking powder

½ tsp (2 mL) baking soda

½ tsp (2 mL) sea salt

¼ tsp (1 mL) ground cardamom

⅓ cup (80 mL) unsalted butter at room temperature

1 cup (250 mL) brown sugar

1 cup (250 mL) mashed ripe banana

1 large egg

1 tsp (5 mL) vanilla extract

1 cup (250 mL) bittersweet chocolate chips

½ cup (120 mL) dried cherries, finely chopped

½ cup (120 mL) unsweetened flaked coconut

4 rings dried pineapple, chopped

½ cup (120 mL) chopped macadamia nuts

BREAKFAST BANANA SMOOTHIE

MAKES 2½ CUPS (600 ML)

2 large frozen bananas, peeled

1 cup (250 mL) vanilla yogurt

½ cup (120 mL) freshly squeezed orange juice

¼ cup (60 mL) quick-cooking rolled oats

2 tbsp (30 mL) good-tasting nutritional yeast

4 ice cubes, crushed

½ tsp (2 mL) vanilla extract

You need to freeze the peeled bananas the night before. They add a depth of flavor that makes this smoothie rich in banana taste and very satisfying.

1. In a blender, combine the bananas, yogurt, orange juice, oats, yeast, ice, and vanilla; blend at high speed for 2 minutes or until the ice has melted.

MANGO BANANA POPSICLES

MAKES 8 SERVINGS

Everyone enjoys a popsicle. They are so easy to make. You can vary the juice (papaya, guava, pineapple) for a refreshing treat on a hot day.

....

1. In a blender or food processor, blend together the mango and orange juices, bananas, and figs until smooth.

2. Pour into 8 popsicle molds. Freeze for 3 hours or until frozen.

1 cup (250 mL) mango juice

½ cup (120 mL) freshly squeezed orange juice

2 medium-size ripe bananas

2 large figs, fresh or dried

BANANA AND KIWI MINI PANCAKES

MAKES 20 MINI PANCAKES

½ cup (120 mL) 2% cottage cheese

½ cup (120 mL) 2% plain
or fruit-flavored yogurt
(to match berries, if using)

1 small ripe banana, puréed
+ 1 small ripe banana, halved
lengthwise and thinly sliced

1 medium-size ripe kiwi,
puréed + 1 ripe kiwi, quartered
lengthwise and thinly sliced

1 large egg

1 tbsp (15 mL) maple syrup

½ tsp (2 mL) vanilla extract

Pinch salt

½ cup (120 mL) unbleached
white flour

½ tsp (2 mL) baking powder

3 tbsp (45 mL) olive oil,
divided

This is a kid-friendly recipe. Easy to prepare and a great way to use up leftover cottage cheese. You can use blueberries, strawberries, or raspberries in place of the kiwi.

....

1. In a food processor, combine the cottage cheese, yogurt, banana purée, kiwi purée, egg, maple syrup, vanilla, and salt; purée until smooth. Transfer to a medium-size bowl.

2. In a large bowl, combine the flour and baking powder; add the cottage cheese mixture until just combined. Gently stir in the sliced banana and kiwi.

3. In a nonstick skillet, heat 1 tbsp (15 mL) oil over medium-high heat. Using 1 tbsp (15 mL) batter for each pancake and the remaining oil as necessary, drop batter onto the skillet. Cook for 3 minutes or until bottom is golden and bubbles break on top. Turn and cook for 3 minutes or until bottom is golden brown.

CURRIED BANANA RUM PIE

MAKES 8 SERVINGS

I don't cook with spirits often but the addition of dark rum to this recipe elevates the flavor of the bananas so well. Fair trade curry powder is a must!

....

1. Preheat oven to 350°F (180°C). Put oven rack in the middle position. Lightly oil a 9-inch (23 cm) pie plate.

2. In a medium-size bowl, stir together the graham cracker crumbs, 2 tbsp (30 mL) sugar, butter, curry powder, and cinnamon with a fork until well-combined. Press the crumb mixture evenly onto the bottom and sides of the pie plate. Bake crust for 10 minutes, then cool in the pie plate on a rack for 15 minutes.

3. In a medium-size bowl, beat together the cream cheese, zest, and remaining brown sugar with an electric mixer at high speed, until light and fluffy, about 1 minute.

4. In a medium-size bowl, beat the cream with the rum at medium speed until it holds soft peaks. Gently stir ⅓ cup (80 mL) whipped cream into the cream cheese mixture, then fold in the remaining whipped cream mixture.

5. Thinly slice the bananas and arrange evenly over the bottom of the crust. Spread cream filling over the bananas, then sprinkle the ginger crumbs over top.

6. Chill pie, covered, for 30 minutes.

1½ cups (350 mL) graham cracker crumbs

½ cup (120 mL) packed muscovado brown sugar, divided

⅓ cup (80 mL) unsalted butter, melted

1 tsp (5 mL) curry powder

¼ tsp (1 mL) ground cinnamon

8 oz (227 g) cream cheese, softened

1 tsp (5 mL) finely grated fresh orange zest

1 cup (250 mL) chilled whipping cream

4 tsp (20 mL) dark rum

3 large ripe bananas

2 tbsp (30 mL) ginger cookie crumbs

BANANA PECAN MUFFINS

MAKES 12 MUFFINS

¾ cup (180 mL) soft whole wheat pastry flour

1 cup (250 mL) unbleached white flour

½ cup (120 mL) packed brown sugar

1 tsp (5 mL) baking powder

1 tsp (5 mL) ground cinnamon

½ tsp (2 mL) baking soda

¼ tsp (1 mL) sea salt

2 ripe bananas, well mashed (about ⅔ cup/160 mL)

¾ cup (180 mL) maple syrup + ¼ tsp (1 mL) extra for brushing

½ cup + 1 tbsp (135 mL) milk

2 large eggs

3 tbsp (45 mL) olive oil

1 tsp (5 mL) apple cider vinegar

½ tsp (2 mL) vanilla extract

½ cup (120 mL) pecans, coarsely chopped

These banana muffins are luscious and a great way to use up that last overripe banana. Use any nut available—almond, walnut, or hazelnut.

1. Preheat oven to 400°F (200°C). Line a 12-cup muffin pan with paper muffin cups.

2. In a large bowl, add the pastry flour, white flour, sugar, baking powder, cinnamon, baking soda, and salt. Stir with a wire whisk to distribute the ingredients.

3. In a medium-size bowl, combine the bananas, maple syrup, milk, eggs, oil, vinegar, and vanilla, and mix until blended. Pour into the dry mixture and stir until the batter is smooth. Stir the pecans into the batter.

4. Fill the prepared muffin cups two-thirds full.

5. Bake for 15 minutes. Brush each muffin top with ¼ tsp (1 mL) maple syrup. Cool on a wire rack for 10 minutes.

BANANA ALMOND NUT BUTTER QUESADILLAS

MAKES 4 SERVINGS

This cooked banana mixture tastes great on toast, on a rice cake, in a sandwich, or wrapped in a tortilla. Cashew or peanut butter is just as delicious.

....

1. Preheat oven to 300°F (150°C). Line a rimmed baking sheet with parchment paper.

2. In a medium-size bowl, toss together the bananas, cherries, lime juice, ginger, chili, and allspice.

3. In a small skillet, warm tortillas over medium-high heat for 2 minutes, turning once. Transfer to the baking sheet and keep warm in the oven.

4. Working with 1 tortilla at a time, place 2 tbsp (30 mL) almond butter down the center of the tortilla. Spoon ½ cup (120 mL) banana mixture over top of the nut butter. Sprinkle with 2 tsp (10 mL) almonds or pecans.

5. Top with another 6-inch (15 cm) tortilla and bake in the oven for 10 minutes. Cut the tortilla in half or quarters to eat.

3 ripe bananas, sliced diagonally, ½ inch (1 cm) thick

3 tbsp (45 mL) dried cherries or cranberries

2 tbsp (30 mL) freshly squeezed lime or lemon juice

1 tsp (5 mL) freshly grated ginger

1 tsp (5 mL) seeded, minced fresh green chili

¼ tsp (1 mL) ground allspice

Eight 6-inch (15 cm) corn or flour tortillas

½ cup (120 mL) smooth almond nut butter

¼ cup (60 mL) almonds or pecans, coarsely chopped

CARAMELIZED BANANAS WITH VANILLA ICE CREAM AND CHOCOLATE SAUCE

MAKES 4 SERVINGS

Bittersweet chocolate served with caramelized bananas, vanilla ice cream, and a hot chocolate sauce. This dessert is rich, gooey, and very satisfying.

¼ cup (60 mL) unsalted butter

4 small firm ripe bananas, sliced diagonally, ½ inch (1 cm) thick

½ cup (120 mL) brown sugar

1¼ cups (300 mL) whipping cream

5 oz (140 g) bittersweet chocolate, finely chopped

Pinch sea salt

1 pint (480 mL) vanilla ice cream

½ cup (120 mL) chopped pecans, toasted and cooled

1. Melt the butter in a 12-inch (30 cm) skillet over medium heat. Add the bananas and sprinkle with brown sugar. Increase heat to medium-high and cook the bananas, turning once and shaking the skillet often until the sugar is caramelized, 2 to 4 minutes.

2. Divide bananas among 4 bowls, leaving any remaining caramelized sugar in the skillet.

3. Add the cream to the skillet and boil over medium heat, whisking until the caramel is dissolved.

4. Add the chocolate with a pinch of sea salt and whisk until melted.

5. Top the bananas with a scoop of ice cream, then drizzle with chocolate sauce and sprinkle with nuts. Use the extra sauce to pour over future bowls of ice cream.

GRILLED BANANA FRUIT KEBOBS

MAKES 8 SKEWERS

3 tbsp (45 mL) olive oil

3 tbsp (45 mL) fresh lime juice

2 tsp (10 mL) ground cinnamon

2 tsp (10 mL) honey

1 firm apple, cut into 8 cubes

1 medium-size firm plum, cut into 8 pieces

2 ripe bananas, each cut into 8 pieces

1 firm pear, cut into 8 cubes

1 firm peach, cut into 8 pieces

Sixteen 1-inch (2.5 cm) chunks pineapple (fresh or canned and drained)

This is a delicious grilled dessert or snack. You can serve one or two per person, depending on the number of people in your group. Grilling the fruit allows the natural sugars to provide most of the flavor. You can use a gas or charcoal grill outdoors or a stovetop grill indoors.

....

1. You will require eight 10-inch (25 cm) wooden or metal skewers. If using wooden skewers, soak them in water for 30 minutes beforehand to prevent scorching. Place the wooden skewers in a water bottle filled with water for an easy soak.

2. Preheat gas grill to medium-high.

3. Stir together the oil, lime juice, cinnamon, and honey in a bowl.

4. Place fruit on each skewer in this order: apple, plum, banana, pear, peach, pineapple, apple, plum, banana, pear, peach, pineapple.

5. Brush kebobs with the oil mixture and place on the grill rack. Grill, turning often, for 10 minutes, or until fruit begins to brown. Baste the grilled fruit with a fruit dipping sauce of your choice. (Recipe for mango dipping sauce on the next page.)

USING A STOVETOP GRILL Use a cast iron or heavy grilling pan to grill kabobs indoors on a stovetop. Heat the grilling pan to sizzling hot over medium-high heat. Once the grilling pan is hot, reduce heat to medium-low. Place skewers on the grill and cook for 10 to 12 minutes, turning skewers as fruit browns.

GRILLED BANANA FRUIT KEBOBS CONTINUED . . .

MANGO LIME JUICE DIPPING SAUCE

MAKES 1 CUP (250 ML)

The perfect sauce to baste cooked fruit kebobs. Sweet and citrusy, it complements the kebobs very well.

3 cups (700 mL) mango juice

¼ cup (60 mL) fresh lime juice

....

1. Bring mango juice to a boil in a medium-size saucepan over medium-high heat. Reduce heat to low and simmer for 45 to 55 minutes until the juice is reduced to 1 cup (250 mL). Let cool and add the lime juice.

2. Use a basting brush to coat the grilled fruit kebobs before serving.

TIP: The dipping sauce can be made ahead and frozen.

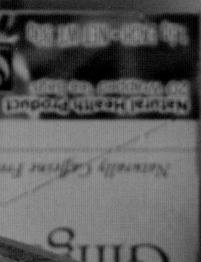

Cha's
ORGANICS

NUTMEG
NOIX DE MUSCADE

WHOLE / ENTIER

Ging

Naturally Saffron

org

Created by

Natural Health Product

Cha's
ORGANICS

ORGANIC
COCONUT MILK

FAIR TRADE  NON-GMO

PREMIUM

GLUTEN FREE
SULPHITE FREE
UNSWEETENED

fair
for life
fair trade

BPA
SANS
BPA

1%
FOR THE
ELEPHANTS

K

SANS GLUTEN
SANS SULFITES
NON SUCRÉ

400 mL

NATURAL SEPARATION MAY OCCUR
SHAKE WELL BEFORE OPENING
SOAK FIRST IN WARM WATER IF SOLID

CANADA ORGANIC · BIOLOGIQUE

Imported

400 mL

Chapter Two

FAIR TRADE
COCONUT MILK

FAIR TRADE
COCONUT MILK

Cha's Organic Coconut Milk

Name of producer co-op:
SOFA (Small Organic Farmers Association).

Location:
Matale, Central Province, Sri Lanka.

How did Cha's Organics connect with SOFA?
My husband, Chanaka, met with them when providing translation services
for a group of Japanese tea importers.

How many members?
Over 3,500 farmer families.

How many years in existence?
The first families joined in 1996, organic certification was obtained in 1997,
and Fairtrade certification was obtained in 1998.

How much food is grown in a season?
As they grow many different crops for local consumption and export, this is
difficult to accurately answer.

How is the crop harvested? Manually or with machines?
Manually.

Where is it sold?
North America, Europe, Japan, and Sri Lanka.

How have the farmers benefited from being a member of Fair for Life?
By receiving a fair price for their crops, in addition to the Fairtrade Premium,
the entire community benefits. You can read about some of the advantages
here: https://sofasl.org/social-economic-developments.

What are SOFA's future plans?

To continue growing and strengthening the small-scale farmer community in Sri Lanka with increasing focus on education and empowerment.

Cha's Organics is a Montreal-based brand of fairly traded organic products that was founded in 2006 by Chanaka Kurera and Marise May. Offering an array of coconut milk and cream, spices, curries, warming beverages, and more, sourced from small- and medium-scale growers from Sri Lanka, Cha's Organics is a leader in the fair trade movement and an innovator in Canadian health food categories.

Chanaka and Marise met while living in Tokyo, far from their native lands of Sri Lanka and Canada, respectively, and soon decided to spend their lives together and to create a family business around bringing the best of Sri Lankan culture and healing foods to Canadians.

Valuing the people who grow their spices, coconuts, and other products has always been a top priority for Cha's Organics. After settling down in Canada, Chanaka and Marise began sourcing these products from the Small Organic Farmers Association (SOFA), the first Fairtrade-certified spice producer group in the world and a partner to this day.

Since then, they have expanded to include a variety of other products, all sourced from organic growers in Sri Lanka including SOFA and other fair trade producer groups who practice traditional agricultural methods and regenerative land management practices. Through their 1% For the Elephants Fund, they also donate 1% of all coconut milk and cream sales to organizations that help protect wild elephants in Sri Lanka.

Visit www.chasorganics.com to learn more.

CHAI RICE PUDDING

MAKES 6 SERVINGS

2 cups (480 mL) water

4 cups (950 mL) coconut milk, divided

2 tsp (10 mL) black chai tea (about 3 tea bags)

1¼ cup (300 mL) basmati rice, rinsed

⅓ cup (80 mL) brown sugar

½ tsp (2 mL) sea salt

1 large apple, cored and diced into small pieces

1 cup (250 mL) fresh or frozen mango pieces, cut into ½-inch (1 cm) sections

1 cup (250 mL) fresh or frozen blueberries

½ cup (120 mL) dried cherries, chopped

½ tsp (2 mL) ground cinnamon

If you like chai tea, you will enjoy this creamy, delicious dessert full of apples, mangoes, blueberries, and dried cherries. Chai tea is made from aromatic spices—cinnamon, cloves, cardamom pods, grated ginger, and black tea. Decaffeinated chai tea bags are available as well. You can use regular, coconut, soy, almond, rice, or hemp milk.

1. In a large saucepan over high heat, bring the water and 2 cups (480 mL) coconut milk to a boil. Remove from heat and add the tea bags. Cover and steep for 3 to 5 minutes. Remove the tea bags.

2. Return saucepan to the stove. Add the rice, sugar, and salt. Stir. Bring to a boil over medium heat. Reduce heat, cover, and simmer for 8 to 10 minutes.

3. Add the remaining 2 cups (480 mL) coconut milk and simmer, uncovered, for 15 minutes, or until rice is cooked.

4. Stir in the apple, mango, blueberries, cherries, and cinnamon. Remove from heat. Cover saucepan and let sit for 10 minutes. Serve warm or at room temperature.

COCONUT GRANOLA

MAKES 8 CUPS (2 L)

Such a satisfying breakfast-on-the-run choice. I always pack a little bag when traveling by plane or car. Much better alternative to salty chips or stale cookies.

....

1. Preheat oven to 325°F (160°C). Line a large rimmed baking sheet with parchment paper.

2. In a large bowl, stir together the oats, coconut, pecans, pumpkin seeds, sunflower seeds, sesame seeds, cinnamon, and cardamom.

3. In a small bowl, combine the oil and maple syrup. Stir to combine. Add to the oat, nut, and seed mixture.

4. Turn the mixture onto the prepared baking sheet and spread in an even layer.

5. Bake until fragrant and golden brown, about 30 to 35 minutes.

6. Remove from oven and let cool on the baking sheet. Once cool, transfer to a large bowl.

7. Stir in the cranberries and ginger.

8. Store in an airtight container for 3 weeks.

4 cups (950 mL) large-flaked rolled oats

1 cup (250 mL) unsweetened coconut

½ cup (120 mL) pecans, chopped

½ cup (120 mL) raw unsalted pumpkin seeds

½ cup (120 mL) raw unsalted sunflower seeds

¼ cup (60 mL) tan sesame seeds

¼ cup (60 mL) black sesame seeds

1 tsp (5 mL) ground cinnamon

¼ tsp (1 mL) ground cardamom

½ cup (120 mL) melted coconut oil

½ cup (120 mL) pure maple syrup

½ cup (120 mL) dried cranberries

¼ cup (60 mL) chopped crystallized ginger

ZUCCHINI COCONUT MUFFINS

MAKES 12 MUFFINS

2 cups (480 mL) all-purpose flour

¼ cup (60 mL) unsweetened shredded coconut

2 tsp (10 mL) ground ginger

1 tsp (5 mL) baking powder

1 tsp (5 mL) ground cinnamon

½ tsp (2 mL) baking soda

½ tsp (2 mL) sea salt

2 large eggs

¾ cup (180 mL) maple syrup

½ cup (120 mL) coconut oil

½ cup (120 mL) coconut milk

1½ cups (350 mL) shredded zucchini (green and yellow) with peel

What do you do when your favorite farmer drops off 5 lbs (2 kg) of just-picked zucchini? Why, you prepare zucchini muffins!

....

1. Preheat oven to 350°F (180°C). Line a standard 12-cup muffin tin with paper liners.

2. In a medium-size bowl, whisk together the flour, coconut, ginger, baking powder, cinnamon, baking soda, and salt.

3. In a small bowl, whisk together the eggs, maple syrup, oil, and milk.

4. Pour the wet ingredients over the flour mixture, sprinkle with zucchini, and stir until batter is combined.

5. Pour ⅓ cup (80 mL) batter into each prepared cup. Bake in the center of the oven for 22 to 25 minutes.

6. Transfer to a wire rack and cool.

CHOCOLATE COCONUT CAKE

MAKES 12 SERVINGS

You will need a hammer to break the chocolate into chunks. Leave the chocolate in its wrapper and it will be easier to gather. This is my favorite cake to take to a potluck. It has a little bit of everything—chocolate, dried cherries, coconut milk.

....

1. Preheat oven to 350°F (180°C).

2. Butter or oil a 9-inch (23 cm) cake pan with 2-inch (5 cm) high sides. Dust pan with flour; set aside.

3. In a medium-size bowl, whisk the flour, baking powder, and sea salt. Stir in ¾ cup (180 mL) coconut.

4. In a large bowl, beat the sugar and butter until light and fluffy. Add the eggs one at a time, beating well.

5. Add the dried cherries and vanilla. Stir well.

6. Add the flour mixture in 2 additions to the sugar–butter mixture. Add the coconut milk, beating just until blended. Fold in half the bittersweet chocolate pieces.

7. Spread the batter evenly in the prepared cake pan. Chop the remaining chocolate into smaller pieces and distribute over the batter. Sprinkle with the remaining coconut.

8. Bake for 40 minutes. If the coconut on top of the cake browns too quickly, cover it with a sheet of aluminum foil.

9. Let cool in the pan.

1¾ cups (415 mL) unbleached white flour + extra for dusting

2 tsp (10 mL) baking powder

1 tsp (5 mL) sea salt

1¼ cups (300 mL) unsweetened shredded coconut, divided

¾ cup (180 mL) brown sugar (muscovado)

½ cup (120 mL) unsalted butter at room temperature

2 large eggs

¼ cup (60 mL) finely chopped dried cherries

1 tsp (5 mL) vanilla extract

One 14-oz (398 mL) can coconut milk

7 oz (200 g) bittersweet chocolate, coarsely chopped, divided

COCONUT CURRY CHOWDER

MAKES 4 TO 6 SERVINGS

6 tbsp (90 mL) coconut
oil, divided

2 tbsp (30 mL) salted butter

Three 6-inch (15 cm) cod fillets,
sliced into 1½-inch (4 cm) pieces

1 medium-size onion, finely diced

1½ tbsp (22 mL) curry powder

2 cups (480 mL) coconut water

2 cups (480 mL) coconut milk

2 cups (480 mL) vegetable broth

2 medium-size carrots, shredded

1 large potato, with peel on, diced
into 1-inch (2.5 cm) pieces

3 cups (700 mL) broccoli
florets, cut into 1-inch
(2.5 cm) pieces

Coconut water is the clear liquid found inside young, green coconuts. It is a delicious substitute for water. I often use it in stir-fry recipes and to cook rice or other grains. You can double the amount of coconut water in this recipe and omit the vegetable stock.

....

1. In a large skillet, heat 3 tbsp (45 mL) coconut oil and melt butter over medium-high heat. Add the fish and cook for 3 to 5 minutes on each side or until fish turns opaque and flakes easily with a fork. Set aside.

2. In a large saucepan or wok, heat the remaining 3 tbsp (45 mL) oil over medium-high heat. Sauté the onion for 5 minutes or until soft. Add the curry powder and cook, stirring constantly, for 1 minute.

3. Add the coconut water, remaining coconut milk, and vegetable broth, and bring to a boil. Add the carrots and potato. Cook for 10 minutes. Add the broccoli.

4. Reduce heat to medium and simmer for 20 minutes, or until vegetables are tender crisp. Ladle into 6 bowls.

5. Divide the fillets in half and add to the bowls.

SWEET POTATO AND COCONUT MILK SOUP

MAKES 8 CUPS (2 L)

Sweet potatoes or squash blend well with coconut milk. Such a velvety taste. Look for well-shaped sweet potatoes with a smooth skin. In a hurry? You can buy peeled, diced sweet potatoes at your local grocery store. They freeze well, too.

....

1. Add enough water to reach the bottom of a collapsible steamer set in a 4-quart (4 L) saucepan and bring to a boil over high heat. Place the sweet potatoes in steamer basket, cover, and steam for 10 to 12 minutes, or until tender.

   Alternately, cover the sweet potatoes with water in a saucepan, bring the water to a boil, reduce heat, and gently boil for 10 to 15 minutes, or until tender.

2. In a large pot, heat the oil over medium heat. Add the onion, salt, and pepper, and cook for 5 minutes, or until softened.

3. Slowly whisk in the stock. Add the coconut milk. Whisk to combine.

4. Add the steamed sweet potatoes. Cook for 5 minutes.

5. Transfer in batches to a food processor or blender. Process until smooth. Return to the pot over medium heat. Add the nutmeg. Stir.

6. Serve and garnish bowls with parsley.

3 cups (700 mL) sweet potatoes cut into 1-inch (2.5 cm) pieces (2 large sweet potatoes)

2 tbsp (30 mL) olive or coconut oil

1½ cups (350 mL) Vidalia onion, diced

1 tsp (5 mL) sea salt

½ tsp (2 mL) ground black pepper

4 cups (950 mL) vegetable stock or water

2 cups (480 mL) coconut milk

½ cup (120 mL) fresh parsley, chopped

½ tsp (2 mL) ground nutmeg

2 tbsp (30 mL) parsley, finely chopped

STRAWBERRY KIWI DESSERT SUSHI

MAKES 4 ROLLS, 24 PIECES

1 cup (250 mL) sushi rice or brown rice, rinsed

2 cups (480 mL) coconut milk

1 tsp (5 mL) mirin

2 tsp (10 mL) wasabi powder or paste

4 to 6 sheets nori (in case a sheet tears)

½ cup (120 mL) strawberries, rinsed and thinly sliced

2 ripe kiwis, peeled and thinly sliced

1 small ripe avocado, thinly sliced, sprinkled with 1 tsp (5 mL) lemon juice

¼ cup (60 mL) pickled sushi ginger, thinly sliced + extra for serving

¼ cup (60 mL) water

Soy sauce for serving

What an incredible dessert! So refreshing. You can mix and match your fruit. Make sure you thinly slice the fruit you use; it is very easy to tear nori if your ingredients are not all the same size.

1. Rinse the rice well in a fine mesh strainer.

2. In a medium-size pot, bring the coconut milk to a boil; add the mirin and rice. Return to a boil. Cover and simmer on low heat for 15 minutes, or until liquid is absorbed.

3. Remove the rice from the pot and place on a rimmed baking sheet lined with parchment paper to cool.

4. Mix the wasabi powder with 3 tsp (15 mL) water to form a paste.

5. Place 1 nori sheet (shiny side down) on a bamboo sushi mat.

6. Spoon ⅓ cup (80 mL) warm rice onto the nori sheet. Leave a 1-inch (2.5 cm) strip of nori uncovered along the top and bottom. Press rice firmly with your fingers or the back of a fork to cover nori sheet, or concentrate rice in one section, lying flat.

7. Place a line of wasabi paste in the middle of the rice. Add a line of sushi ginger. Place 4 to 6 strips of fruit and avocado evenly across the rice.

8. To roll, lift the sushi mat (at the edge closest to you) and begin to roll up, holding the filling in place with your index fingers. Roll the nori, neatly and firmly, like a jelly roll, almost to the end. Using a fingertip, moisten the top strip of nori with some water to seal the roll. Cut each roll into 6 pieces.

9. Serve with extra sushi ginger slices, wasabi paste, and good-quality soy sauce.

POPPY SEED COCONUT MILK CAKE

MAKES 12 SERVINGS

Soaking poppy seeds in full-fat coconut milk is decadent, and this cake has such a smooth, rich flavor. Not too sweet, a little dense, and so satisfying. This fair trade full-fat coconut milk from Sri Lanka is fantastic: Cha's Organics.

....

1. Preheat oven to 350°F (180°C). Butter and flour a 10-inch (25 cm) Bundt pan; set aside.

2. Combine 1⅓ cups (320 mL) coconut milk with the poppy seeds and 1 tsp (5 mL) lemon zest in a small pot. Bring to a boil. Remove from heat and allow to steep for 20 minutes in the pot. Let cool.

3. In a large bowl, whisk the flour, baking powder, and salt.

4. In a medium-size bowl, cream together the butter, honey, and sugar with an electric mixer. Beat in the eggs, vanilla, the remaining coconut milk, as well as the remaining zest. Add the cooled poppy seed mixture.

5. Add the butter–poppy seed mixture to the dry ingredients. Stir until combined.

6. Pour into the prepared pan. Bake 40 to 45 minutes or until a toothpick comes out clean. Allow to cool in the pan for 10 minutes. Invert onto a cooling rack; let cool.

2 cups (480 mL) full-fat coconut milk, divided

1 cup (250 mL) poppy seeds

1 tbsp (15 mL) lemon zest, divided

2 cups (480 mL) unbleached white flour

1 tbsp (15 mL) baking powder

½ tsp (2 mL) sea salt

½ cup (120 mL) unsalted butter at room temperature

½ cup (120 mL) honey

½ cup (120 mL) brown sugar

2 large eggs

1 tsp (5 mL) vanilla extract

ALMOND MACAROON TART

MAKES 16 BITE-SIZE PIECES

CRUST

1½ cups (350 mL) unbleached white flour

¾ cup (180 mL) unsweetened finely shredded coconut

½ cup (120 mL) packed brown sugar

½ tsp (2 mL) sea salt

½ cup (120 mL) unsalted butter, melted

FILLING

1 cup (250 mL) unsweetened finely shredded coconut

¼ cup (60 mL) brown sugar

3 large egg whites

6 oz (170 g) blackberries, halved

4 oz (115 g) blueberries, rinsed

3 tbsp (45 mL) almonds, toasted and chopped

The perfect bite. For coconut lovers. Lots of fruit to choose from, fresh or frozen. Use strawberries, kiwi, or grapes, thinly sliced and in small pieces.

....

1. Preheat oven to 350°F (180°C). Grease an 8- × 11-inch (20 × 28 cm) tart pan and line bottom and sides with parchment paper.

CRUST

2. In large bowl, combine the flour, coconut, sugar, and salt.

3. Using a fork, stir in the melted butter until the dough is crumbly.

4. Firmly press into the bottom of the prepared pan.

5. Bake for about 15 minutes, or until barely golden. Let cool on a rack.

FILLING

6. Mix the coconut, sugar, and egg whites in a small bowl until well-combined.

7. Evenly arrange the blackberries and blueberries on the cooled crust.

8. Spoon the coconut filling over the berries; gently spread it over the berries, leaving some of the berries exposed.

9. Bake 20 to 25 minutes or until golden. Let cool completely on a rack.

10. Garnish with almonds before serving.

MAPLE SYRUP APPLE PIE

MAKES 8 SERVINGS

I adore a baked apple. But baking apples for a pie is the ultimate dessert. Serve with vanilla ice cream or just plain.

....

ROASTED APPLE FILLING

1. Preheat oven to 400°F (200°C)

2. Line a rimmed baking sheet with parchment paper.

3. In a large bowl, toss together the apples, cinnamon, cardamom, maple syrup, and lemon juice. Spread evenly on the baking sheet.

4. Bake for 30 minutes.

CRUST

5. Preheat oven to 350°F (180°C).

6. In a food processor, blend together the flour, baking powder, and salt. Add the coconut oil, maple syrup, and vanilla. Pulse until completely combined. Slowly add the water and pulse until a slightly moist dough is formed.

7. Wrap dough in plastic wrap and refrigerate for 20 minutes.

8. Place a sheet of parchment paper on the work surface. Heavily sprinkle with flour.

9. Place the unwrapped dough on the paper and sprinkle with flour. Using a rolling pin, roll out the dough. Brush off excess flour and fit into a 10-inch (25 cm) pie plate, letting excess dough hang over the rim of the plate. Trim the excess dough away and discard.

10. Fill the pie shell with the roasted apple filling and spread evenly.

11. Place pie on a baking sheet and bake on the bottom rack for 30 minutes.

12. Let the pie cool on a rack for 10 minutes before serving. Store the pie at room temperature, covered, for up to 3 days.

ROASTED APPLE FILLING

1 lb (454 g) Spy, Empire, or Fuji apples, peeled, cored, and diced into 1-inch (2.5 cm) pieces

1 lb (454 g) green apples, peeled, cored, and diced into 1-inch (2.5 cm) pieces

½ tsp (2 mL) ground cinnamon

½ tsp (2 mL) ground cardamom

¼ cup (60 mL) maple syrup

2 tbsp (30 mL) fresh lemon juice

CRUST

2 cups (480 mL) all-purpose flour

4 tsp (20 mL) baking powder

¾ tsp (4 mL) sea salt

½ cup (120 mL) coconut oil

½ cup (120 mL) maple syrup

2 tsp (10 mL) vanilla extract

7 tbsp (105 mL) cold water

COCOA CASHEW COCONUT BALLS

MAKES 24 BALLS

¼ cup (60 mL) unsalted
butter, melted

½ cup (120 mL) maple syrup

¼ cup (60 mL) milk (soy, almond,
or dairy)

3 tbsp (45 mL) cocoa powder,
unsweetened

½ tsp (2 mL) vanilla

1½ cups (350 mL) small
rolled oats

¼ cup (60 mL) cashew nut butter

1 cup (250 mL) shredded coconut,
unsweetened

What a great snack. Not too sweet. Satisfying and just the right size. You can use any nut butter that is available, peanut or almond. Nuts to You is my favorite brand.

1. In a small saucepan, melt the butter. Add the maple syrup, milk, cocoa, and vanilla. Stir with a whisk. Bring to a boil, stirring often. Allow to cool.

2. In a medium-size bowl, combine the oats and cashew nut butter.

3. Pour the cocoa mixture over the oat mixture. Stir well. Add the coconut.

4. Using your hands, roll the dough into 1-inch (2.5 cm) balls. They will be sticky but will harden as they cool.

GINGERBREAD STRIPS

MAKES TWENTY-FOUR 2-INCH (5 CM) STRIPS

Molasses makes all the difference in this recipe. When combined with dark brown sugar, the taste is sweet but has a depth not found in ordinary gingerbread. The sugar slightly caramelizes and is so tasty. These delicious strips can be bookends for an ice cream sandwich or your new moist snack.

....

1. Preheat the oven to 350°F (180°C).

2. Line a rimmed baking sheet with parchment paper.

3. In a medium-size bowl, whisk the flour with ginger, cinnamon, cloves, baking soda, and salt.

4. In a large bowl, cream the butter with 1 cup (250 mL) brown sugar and granulated sugar, until fluffy. Stir in the molasses. Beat in the eggs, one at a time.

5. Add the flour–spice mixture in 3 additions and beat to blend.

6. Spread the batter onto the prepared baking sheet. Sprinkle the remaining brown sugar over top of the batter.

7. Bake the gingerbread for 20 to 25 minutes, or until golden brown. Cool in the pan on a cooling rack.

8. Cut crosswise into 4 equal strips; cut each strip into 6 pieces for 24 strips.

2 cups (480 mL) all-purpose flour

2¼ tsp (11 mL) ground ginger

1 tsp (5 mL) ground cinnamon

¼ tsp (1 mL) ground cloves

½ tsp (2 mL) baking soda

½ tsp (2 mL) salt

½ cup (120 mL) unsalted butter at room temperature

1¼ cups (300 mL) lightly packed dark brown sugar, divided

¼ cup (60 mL) granulated sugar

¼ cup (60 mL) fancy molasses

2 large eggs

BARLEY MISO RICE NOODLE BOWL

MAKES 6 SERVINGS

Cha's Organics has a superb line of coconut milks, one of which is lemongrass-flavored. If not available, add 2 tbsp (30 mL) diced lemongrass to your plain coconut milk. This soup is so welcome at the end of a long day. Refreshing and filling, the combination of miso and noodles is so satisfying.

....

1. Heat the oil in a wok or large saucepan over medium heat. Add the onion and cook until softened, about 4 minutes. Add the mushrooms and red peppers; cook 2 minutes. Add the celery, kale leaves, and 3 tbsp (45 mL) water or stock. Cook until softened, about 3 to 5 minutes.

2. Add the garlic and ginger; stir to combine and cook 2 minutes. Add the coconut milk, miso paste, and 2 cups (480 mL) water; whisk to combine. Heat through, stirring often. Bring to a simmer. Reduce heat and cook for 10 minutes.

3. Meanwhile, prepare the rice noodles as directed on the package.

4. To serve, divide the noodles between 6 soup bowls and ladle soup on top of the noodles.

2 tbsp (30 mL) toasted sesame oil

1 small red onion, thinly sliced

1½ cups (350 mL) thinly sliced shiitake mushrooms

1 cup (250 mL) roasted red peppers, thinly sliced

2 stalks celery, diced

3 cups (700 mL) thinly sliced kale leaves

3 tbsp (45 mL) water or vegetable stock

3 small garlic cloves, minced

1 tbsp (15 mL) minced fresh ginger root

Two 14-oz (398 mL) cans lemongrass coconut milk

¾ cup (180 mL) barley miso paste

2 cups (480 mL) cold water

½ lb (227 g) dry rice noodles

TOFU BAKED FRIES
WITH SHALLOT ALMOND SAUCE

MAKES 4 SERVINGS

12 oz (340 g) extra-firm tofu

2 tbsp (30 mL) coconut oil

½ tsp (2 mL) sea salt

3 tbsp (45 mL) black and tan toasted sesame seeds

I don't deep-fry. Simply browning tofu in an oiled skillet will brown and crisp the tofu nicely. Use black and tan sesame seeds if available.

For info on how to toast seeds, see page 197.

1. Preheat oven to 350°F (180°C). Line a rimmed baking sheet with parchment paper.

2. Using a sharp knife, cut the tofu into 3- × ¼-inch (7½ cm × 6 mm) strips.

3. Place the tofu slices on the baking sheet. Bake for 8 minutes.

4. Heat a large nonstick skillet over medium heat until hot. Add the coconut oil and swirl to coat the pan. Lay the tofu slices in the pan and sprinkle with salt. After 4 minutes, flip the slices over and cook for another 4 minutes. Tofu will be golden.

5. Sprinkle with sesame seeds and cook for about 2 minutes, scraping the bottom of the pan to get up any bits that stick to it.

6. Serve warm with Shallot Almond Sauce, below.

SHALLOT ALMOND SAUCE

MAKES 1¼ CUPS (300 ML)

4 medium shallots, unpeeled

½ cup (120 mL) coconut milk

¼ cup (60 mL) smooth almond nut butter

2 tbsp (30 mL) fresh lime juice

1½ tsp (7 mL) tamari or soy sauce

½ tsp (2 mL) smoked paprika

¼ tsp (1 mL) sea salt

This smooth almond sauce can be used as a dip for Tofu Baked Fries, or as a dressing for noodles, hot or cold. Shallots resemble onions but are not as harsh. Always inspect your shallots—no sprouting or soft spots. They go well with nut butters.

1. Preheat oven to 350°F (180°C). Line a rimmed baking sheet with parchment paper.

2. Roast shallots on the baking sheet for 30 minutes, or until very tender and the juices start to ooze out. Let cool slightly before squeezing the shallots out of their skins into a food processor. Purée.

3. Add the coconut milk, almond butter, lime juice, tamari, smoked paprika, and salt; blend until smooth.

4. Put the mixture into a small saucepan and heat slowly over medium heat, stirring constantly for 5 minutes. Mixture will thicken.

5. Serve warm or at room temperature.

SOBA NOODLE SALAD

MAKES 4 SERVINGS

¼ cup (60 mL) toasted
sesame oil

2 tbsp (30 mL) rice vinegar

2 tbsp (30 mL) soy sauce

2 small garlic cloves, minced

½ tsp (2 mL) minced
fresh ginger root

½ tsp (2 mL) hot pepper sauce

2 cups (480 mL) coconut milk

2 cups (480 mL) water

4 oz (115 g) soba noodles
(a combination of buckwheat and
unbleached white flour)

4 oz (115 g) green beans,
trimmed and halved

¼ cup (60 mL) thinly sliced
red onions

Half an English cucumber, diced

1 carrot, grated

¼ cup (60 mL) dried cherries
or cranberries

½ cup (120 mL) mint leaves,
sliced thinly

½ cup (120 mL) lightly toasted
pine nuts (see page 197)

Not all soba noodles are equal. The 100% buckwheat noodles are an acquired taste. They have a pronounced flavor and texture that is not familiar to people raised on semolina pasta. Sobaya is a Montreal-based pasta company that makes many kinds of soba noodles. The fresh mint and crunch of pine nuts are a great complement to the texture of the noodles.

1. Combine the sesame oil, vinegar, soy sauce, garlic, ginger, and hot pepper sauce in a large bowl; whisk until blended.

2. In a medium-size saucepan, bring the coconut milk and water to a boil. Add the soba noodles and cook according to the package directions. Do not discard the cooking liquid. Using a slotted spoon, add the noodles to the dressing in a large bowl. Toss with tongs.

3. Add the green beans to the cooking liquid in the saucepan and cook for 3 to 5 minutes, or until just tender. Using a slotted spoon, add the beans to the noodles. Mix gently to combine.

4. Add the red onions, cucumber, carrot, and cherries.

5. Stir in the mint and pine nuts.

COCONUT CREAMED CORN

MAKES 4½ CUPS (1.2 L)

If you decide to use frozen corn niblets, increase the cooking time an additional 8 minutes. A great addition to any burrito filling or wrap.

....

1. Combine the corn, coconut milk, and salt in a medium saucepan. Bring to a boil, reduce heat, and simmer, stirring occasionally, for 15 minutes, or until most of the coconut milk has evaporated.

2. Stir in the basil, lime juice, and ancho chili powder.

2 cups (480 mL) thawed frozen corn niblets

1 cup (250 mL) coconut milk

¼ tsp (1 mL) sea salt

3 tbsp (45 mL) chopped fresh basil

1 tbsp (15 mL) fresh lime juice

¼ tsp (1 mL) ancho chili powder

Chapter Three

FAIR TRADE COFFEE

FAIR TRADE
COFFEE

Merchants of Green Coffee

Name of producer co-op:
Birding Coffee; formerly Cooperativa COMISUYL.

Location:
Subirana, Yoro, Honduras.

How did Merchants of Green Coffee connect with Birding Coffee?
The co-op joined the Cafe Solar® program in 2012 with Maira Manzanares as its founder and General Manager (at that time, Merchants of Green Coffee and the Mesoamerican Development Institute [MDI] had already been part-nered in the solar-drying/reforestation program since 1996). Raul Rauddales (from MDI) met Maira at a Fairtrade conference in Guatemala (late 2000s).

How many members are in the co-op?
The new Birding Coffee has 70 to 100 farming families and membership is growing rapidly.

How many years have you been in business?
Birding Coffee is new (2018/19). Cooperativa COMISUYL is now seven years old (since 2012).

How much coffee is grown in a season?
Annual production is based on grower membership, which fluctuates all the time. An average farm is four acres (1.5 hectares) and each farm produces approx. 1,000 to 1,500 lbs (450 to 680 kg) annually. In previous seasons our co-op (COMISUYL) averaged between 200 to 300 growers, and this year's new program (Birding Coffee) has 70 to 100 and growing.

How is the crop harvested? Manually or with machines?
Manually, hand-picked.

Where is it sold?
Direct through Merchants of Green Coffee.

How have the farmers benefited from being a member of Fairtrade? How many years have they been a member of a fair trade co-op?

Both Birding Coffee and Cooperativa COMISUYL have always been Fairtrade-certified. "The benefit of Fairtrade is that it allows producer organizations to provide services (marketing, technical support, processing, export) without going into debt. Also, the Premium is spent on projects that are decided by the members of the organization."–Richard Trubey, Mesoamerican Development Institute

What are the co-op's future plans?

Upgrade the solar-powered processing facility and add four more dryers (expanding production capacity five times to produce millions of pounds of coffee). Increase grower membership. Measure and trade carbon credits accumulated from restorative farming practices (Integrated Open Canopy [IOC] farming). Continued forest mapping, bird research, and work on alternative, renewable biofuel sources that provide additional employment in sustainable farming in the region.

Why I Buy Their Coffee Beans

First of all, their coffee beans are packaged in biodegradable bags made of post-consumer content with a vegetable-based lining. To me, they are the most environmentally responsible form of coffee packaging today.

Coffee naturally oxidizes five to seven days after roasting. MGC has a network of local roasters who roast certified green coffee beans on a weekly basis and deliver the coffee to their location within 24 hours of roasting. Each bag is sealed with its own roast date. You can pick up your coffee or arrange delivery. There is nothing more spectacular than freshly roasted beans. The flavor is so pronounced, especially if you like a dark roast as I do, and there is a velvety, complex berry taste to each cup. I do not finish my 1 lb bag of coffee within the five to seven day period, as my husband Jim does not drink coffee, nor does Emery, my 21 year old son. Still, the taste and aroma of my freshly brewed coffee is far superior to any coffee from a chain store. When I have the time, I roast my own green coffee beans in an electric coffee roaster, 1½ cups (350 mL) at a time. I can also roast nuts this way. I need to be reminded to open the window, as not everyone likes the dense coffee smell. You can buy freshly roasted coffee beans or green beans to roast yourself.

One source of MGC coffee is the Fairtrade-certified female-managed coffee co-op Cooperativa Comisuyl in Honduras. They are pioneering "solar dried" commercial coffee processing. This off-grid technology was created by the Mesoamerican Development Institute (MDI), a nonprofit organization, and uses fully clean, renewable energy from solar panels to dry the coffee quickly. Coffee needs to be dried before it is exported to preserve it, but conventional drying is not environmentally sustainable, with much of the drying process fueled by burning wood from nearby forests. Solar technology can replace the wood burning drying of coffee beans and protect natural tropical forests.

Fairtrade Board of Canada visits Poco Fundo coffee farmers in the state of Minas Gerais, Brazil

BRAZILIAN FAIR TRADE COFFEE CO-OP

I had the opportunity to visit a fair trade coffee producer in the mountainous region of Minas Gerais, Brazil. It was six hours north of San Paolo by car. We visited Poco Fundo, a village of 17,000 inhabitants. The landscape is full of coffee bushes, which constitute the predominant activity of the area. At the time (2016), I was on the board of Fairtrade Canada and my board went to Brazil on an educational mission. We were there with Naji Harb, a Canadian who moved to Brazil and was chair of Fairtrade Brazil.

Minas Gerais is the main producer of Brazilian coffee. In 1991, the small-scale farmers of Poco Fundo organized to found an association of small-scale producers with the objective of improving their own quality of life and work. Seventy-six families united to form the cooperative, determined to increase the productivity of their small plots and sustain the quality of family-oriented agriculture in the area. Called Coopfam, the cooperative became Fairtrade-certified by Fairtrade International in 1998 and began exporting to North America in 2003.

Coopfam is one of 15 Brazilian Fairtrade-certified producer groups that participated in the 2007–2010 Responsible Sourcing Partnership (RSP) project. The RSP project wanted to improve the quality of Brazilian coffee, increase market linkages, and raise producer capacity. Through this project, Coopfam participated in cooperative governance training, cupper and business management training, and post-harvest best practices to improve coffee quality.

Being a member of the Fairtrade network has allowed the co-op to hire agricultural technicians who can give support and training to members and assist in soil analysis, coffee harvesting, and drying programs. The Fairtrade Premium has provided new healthcare services (eye care, dental visits,

Coffee 101

The 3 Keys to the Best Tasting Coffee:

1. Quality Green Beans

2. Freshness of the Roast

3. Proper Brewing

FRESH COFFEE • FAIR

Coffee Tree

2-year-old arabica coffee tree seedling. Coffee is a perennial shrub that, once established, will flower and fruit (cherries), inside which are two coffee beans or "seeds."

1. Quality Green Beans
2. Freshness of the Roast
3. Proper Brewing

and gynecologists) and new administrative improvements. Purchases of computers, printers, and office furniture have improved the working environment and marketing opportunities.

Coopfam owns 300,000 plants of organically grown Arabica coffee, Catuai, and Mundo Novo varietals. As we walked the terrain and met with the farmers, I was impressed with their commitment to avoiding chemical fertilizers and pesticides. The beans are slowly dried in the sun, in a natural way, so that the coffee, as well as being free from pesticides, does not lose the properties acquired with the growth. The result is a drink with characteristics similar to a high-quality coffee from Central America, with an equilibrated acidity.

We were invited to lunch and a coffee cupping. We tasted the coffee beans at several stages of roasting. I like a dark roast. They had hundreds of cups and no dishwasher. There wasn't any cream, milk, or sugar—you didn't need it.

At a cupping, you are given a small amount of coffee to taste; people often spit excess coffee into a bucket and discuss the level of acidity, flavor, aroma, and color. It was fascinating.

COFFEE CUPPING GUIDELINES
Led by Lloyd Bernhardt, a friend to fair trade coffee farmers

REGION: Cerrado, Minas Gerais, Brazil
GROWING ALTITUDE: 875 to 1,200 yards (800 to 1,100 meters)
ARABICA VARIETY: Mundo Novo, Catuai
HARVEST PERIOD: September to March
MILLING PROCESS: Natural
AROMA: Floral
FLAVOR: Berry and tangerine notes
BODY: Velvety, smooth
ACIDITY: Sweet

SUMMARY
Floral aroma, velvety body, smooth, sweet acidity, complex berry and tangerine notes, well-balanced cup.

I bought a few pounds of coffee and it was the first time in my life I had purchased coffee beans that were freshly picked, roasted, and bagged within a matter of days. The flavor was terrific, so fresh and smooth.

I live in Toronto and visit Merchants of Green Coffee for green beans and freshly roasted beans. They are an amazing coffee house with over a dozen types of fair trade coffee beans. Coffee classes are held regularly, and you can educate your palette, buy a coffee roaster, and subscribe to a coffee purchasing plan. Visit www.merchantsofgreencoffee.com for more information.

COFFEE SPICE RUB FLANK STEAK

MAKES 4 SERVINGS

For this recipe, you combine the spices and oil and stir to form a paste that you rub all over the flank steak. You can marinate for a few hours or overnight. My lead recipe tester, Heather, pronounced it delicious.

....

1. Combine the oil, coffee, salt, sugar, paprika, pepper, chili powder, and cumin in a small bowl. Stir to form a paste. Rub the paste all over the steak.

2. Marinate in the fridge for 3 hours or overnight.

3. Place on a greased grill. Cook on medium-high heat for 5 to 6 minutes on each side until medium-rare.

4. Remove from heat. Allow to stand, covered, for 5 minutes. Thinly slice.

2 tbsp (30 mL) olive oil

2 tbsp (30 mL) ground coffee

1 tbsp (15 mL) sea salt

1 tbsp (15 mL) brown sugar

2 tsp (10 mL) smoked paprika

1 tsp (5 mL) black pepper

1 tsp (5 mL) chili powder

1 tsp (5 mL) ground cumin

1 lb (454 g) flank steak

COFFEE CRUSTED FLAT IRON STEAK

MAKES 4 SERVINGS

1 cup (250 mL) espresso
coffee beans

12 garlic cloves, minced

1 cup (250 mL) chopped
fresh herbs (sage, thyme,
flat-leaf parsley)

½ cup (120 mL) cracked black
peppercorns

½ cup (120 mL) extra virgin
olive oil

¼ cup (60 mL) molasses

¼ cup (60 mL) balsamic vinegar

¼ cup (60 mL) brown sugar

Kosher salt to taste

2 lbs (1 kg) beef (rib eye
or tenderloin roast or flat iron
steak, also good with chicken,
lamb, and pork)

My friend Chef Vanessa Yeung from Aphrodite Cooks contributed this coffee rub recipe to the book. As a leading caterer and cooking school owner, she has her pulse on many culinary trends and her food is always delicious.

....

1. Place the coffee beans, garlic, herbs, peppercorns, oil, molasses, vinegar, brown sugar, and salt in a food processor and blend until you have a rough coffee paste.

2. Rub the entire surface of the beef generously with coffee paste; cover, refrigerate, and allow to marinate for 24 hours.

3. Remove the beef and carefully wipe off any excess marinade with a dry towel. Season to taste with salt and freshly ground black pepper.

4. Preheat oven to 450°F (230°C). Place the tenderloin roast on a parchment-lined baking sheet. Roast at high heat for 20 minutes. Reduce heat to 350°F (180°C) and cook for another 25 to 30 minutes, or until the internal temperature reaches 120 to 125°F (50 to 52°C), using a meat thermometer to test for doneness.

5. Before carving, let the beef rest for 10 minutes.

DRIED PAPAYA, CHERRY, BROWN RICE MUFFINS

MAKES 12 TO 14 MUFFINS

These are my favorite type of muffin. Made with whole grains and organically dried fruit, they are such a tasty bite. Not too sweet. Mix and match the dried fruit, depending on what you have in your pantry. Follow the amounts and you will have a great dessert.

....

1. Preheat oven to 400°F (200°C).

2. In a medium-size pot, add 2 cups (480 mL) coconut milk and the cinnamon sticks. Bring to a boil over high heat. Stir in the rinsed rice. Cover, reduce heat, and simmer for 40 to 45 minutes, or until the rice is tender.

3. In a large bowl, mix together the whole wheat and white flours, rolled oats, baking powder, salt, and cardamom.

4. In a medium-size bowl, stir together the remaining 1½ cups (350 mL) coconut milk, oil, and maple syrup. Stir in the cooked brown rice, papaya, apricots, cherries, and walnuts. Mix well.

5. Stir the coconut milk–dried fruit mixture into the dry ingredients. Stir until just moistened.

6. Spoon into 12 large paper cups in a muffin pan. Bake in the oven for 25 minutes, or until a toothpick inserted in the center comes out clean. Cool in the pan for 10 minutes; turn out on a rack and let cool.

3½ cups (830 mL) coconut milk, divided

Two 2-inch (5 cm) cinnamon sticks

1 cup (250 mL) brown rice, rinsed

1½ cups (350 mL) whole wheat pastry flour

1 cup (250 mL) unbleached white flour

¼ cup (60 mL) rolled oats

1 tbsp (15 mL) baking powder

¾ tsp (4 mL) sea salt

½ tsp (2 mL) ground cardamom

1½ cups (350 mL) coconut milk

½ cup (120 mL) olive oil

½ cup (120 mL) maple syrup

½ cup (120 mL) dried papaya, diced

½ cup (120 mL) dried apricots, chopped

½ cup (120 mL) dried cherries or raisins, chopped

½ cup (120 mL) walnuts, chopped

COFFEE VANILLA BANANA LOAF

MAKES 8 TO 10 SERVINGS

I like to use espresso beans for this recipe. They lend a subtle yet distinct taste. I always heat up the leftover coffee and have a cup.

....

1. Preheat oven to 350° F (180°C). Grease a 9- × 5-inch (23 × 13 cm) loaf pan with olive oil; set aside.

2. Place 2 tbsp (30 mL) ground coffee in a coffee filter. Place the filter over a medium-size cup or mug. Pour 1 cup (250 mL) boiling water over the ground coffee. When all the water has dripped down, transfer the coffee in the mug to a medium-size bowl. Add the sliced bananas. Soak in the coffee liquid for 5 minutes. Discard the liquid. Using a large slotted spoon, remove and gently place the bananas on the bottom of the oiled loaf pan in 2 straight rows.

3. In a large bowl, beat the butter with the brown sugar by hand or in a mixer, until light and fluffy. Beat in the egg and vanilla.

4. In a separate bowl, combine the remaining mashed bananas with the yogurt and baking soda. Set aside.

5. Combine the flour with the chocolate chips, remaining ground coffee, walnuts, and baking powder in a separate medium-size bowl.

6. Add the flour and the mashed banana mixture to the butter mixture. Mix well.

7. Scrape into the prepared loaf pan and bake in the oven for 50 to 60 minutes, or until a cake tester inserted into the center of the loaf comes out clean. Let cool in the pan for 10 minutes. Invert onto a cooling rack; let cool.

3 tbsp (45 mL) ground coffee beans, divided

1 cup (250 mL) boiling water

1 banana sliced into fifteen ½-inch (1 cm) pieces + 1½ cups (350 mL) mashed bananas

½ cup (120 mL) salted butter at room temperature, or ½ cup (120 mL) fair trade olive oil

1 cup (250 mL) muscovado brown sugar

1 large egg

1 tsp (5 mL) vanilla extract

½ cup (120 mL) plain Greek yogurt or buttermilk

½ tsp (2 mL) baking soda

1½ cups (350 mL) unbleached white flour

½ cup (120 mL) semisweet chocolate chips

½ cup (120 mL) walnuts, chopped

1 tsp (5 mL) baking powder

CARDAMOM COFFEE

MAKES 2 SERVINGS

¼ cup (60 mL) whole coffee beans or ¼ cup (60 mL) ground coffee beans

6 whole cardamom pods or ¼ tsp (1 mL) ground cardamom per cup

16 oz (480 mL) water

Try adding cardamom to your morning coffee. The combination of peppery sweet cardamom with freshly ground coffee beans is simply delicious.

....

1. Grind the coffee beans and cardamom pods finely in a coffee grinder.

2. Brew the coffee as you normally would.

3. Add your favorite condiments (milk, cream, sugar) or drink black.

TIP: I like to buy vanilla beans, cut them into ¼-inch (6 mm) pieces, and grind the piece of vanilla with coffee beans instead of cardamom pods, for variety.

ESPRESSO GLAZE COFFEE CAKE

MAKES 8 SERVINGS

Instant espresso powder is available in Italian grocery stores and supermarkets. It is made by high-heat drying brewed espresso coffee. The dark, strong coffee flavor comes across so well. Keep in a cool, dark cupboard.

....

1. Preheat oven to 350°F (180°C) and place rack in the middle position. Butter a 10-cup/10-inch (2.5 L/25 cm) Bundt pan.

2. In a medium-size bowl, whisk together the flour, baking powder, baking soda, and salt.

3. In a large bowl, combine the sugar and butter. Beat with an electric mixer at medium speed until pale and fluffy, 2 to 3 minutes. Add the eggs one at a time, beating well with each addition. Beat in the vanilla.

4. Add the flour mixture alternately with yogurt, mixing until combined.

5. Transfer one-third of the batter to a small bowl. Add the espresso mixture and stir until combined.

6. Spoon half the plain batter into the Bundt pan and spread evenly. Top with the coffee batter, spreading it slowly so it evenly covers the plain batter.

7. Cover with the remaining plain batter.

8. Bake for 55 to 60 minutes. Cool in a pan on a rack for 10 minutes. Invert onto a plate to cool completely.

GLAZE

9. Stir together brewed coffee and espresso powder in a medium-size bowl. Add the sugar and stir until well-combined.

10. Pour the glaze over the cake and let stand until the glaze is set, about 10 to 15 minutes.

2 cups (480 mL) all-purpose flour

1 tsp (5 mL) baking powder

½ tsp (2 mL) baking soda

¼ tsp (1 mL) sea salt

1 cup (250 mL) granulated sugar

¾ cup (180 mL) unsalted butter

2 large eggs

1½ tsp (7 mL) vanilla extract

1 cup (250 mL) yogurt

2 tbsp (30 mL) instant espresso powder, dissolved in 1 tbsp (15 mL) boiling water

GLAZE

3 tbsp (45 mL) strong brewed coffee

2 tsp (10 mL) instant espresso powder

1¾ cups (415 mL) confectioners sugar, sifted

BITTERSWEET MOCHA ALMOND BARS

MAKES 16 BARS

This is a bar cookie. Melted chocolate is spread over a baked espresso-toffee base and topped with chopped roasted almonds. Serve with a cup of coffee or tea.

....

1. Preheat oven to 350°F (180°C) and place rack in the middle position.

2. In a large bowl, beat together the butter and brown sugar with an electric mixer at medium-high speed for 3 minutes. Beat in the yolk and vanilla, then add the espresso mixture, beating until well-combined.

3. Add the flour and salt and mix until combined.

4. Spread the dough evenly in a greased, rimmed 8- × 8-inch (20 × 20 cm) baking dish. Bake for 20 minutes or until the top puffs and the sides pull away from the edges of the pan.

5. Melt the chocolate in a small metal bowl set over a small saucepan of hot water, stirring often. Remove bowl from heat.

6. Spread the melted chocolate over the baked dough and sprinkle with almonds. Cool in the pan on a rack.

7. Cut into 16 bars and refrigerate until chocolate is firm, about 20 minutes.

½ cup (120 mL) unsalted butter at room temperature

½ cup (120 mL) packed brown sugar

1 large egg yolk

1 tsp (5 mL) vanilla extract

2 tbsp (30 mL) instant espresso powder, dissolved in 1 tbsp (15 mL) boiling water

1 cup (250 mL) all-purpose flour

¼ tsp (1 mL) salt

4 oz (115 g) bittersweet chocolate, finely chopped

1 cup (250 mL) roasted salted almonds, chopped

ORANGE ZEST CHOCOLATE COFFEE COOKIES

MAKES 12 COOKIES

1½ cups (350 mL)
all-purpose flour

2 tsp (10 mL) ground cinnamon

¼ tsp (1 mL) baking soda

¼ tsp (1 mL) sea salt

½ cup (120 mL) unsalted
butter (1 stick)

1 cup (250 mL) packed
brown sugar

1 tsp (5 mL) vanilla extract

1 tsp (5 mL) grated organic
orange zest

1 large egg

2 tsp (10 mL) instant
espresso powder

6 oz (170 g) dark chocolate,
chopped into chunks

½ cup (120 mL) toasted
walnuts, chopped

The pronounced coffee flavor of these cookies goes so well with the dark chocolate, walnuts, and brown sugar. My husband Jim likes to take these cookies with him for a snack when canoeing on Bella Lake. A good energy boost.

1. Preheat oven to 350°F (180°C). Line a rimmed baking sheet with parchment paper.

2. In a small bowl, mix together the flour, cinnamon, baking soda, and salt.

3. In a large bowl, beat together the butter and brown sugar with an electric mixer at medium speed for 3 minutes. Add the vanilla, zest, egg, and espresso powder, beating until smooth.

4. Add the flour mixture, mixing until just blended. Stir in the chocolate chunks and walnuts.

5. Scoop the dough into scant ¼-cup (60 mL) balls and place on the prepared baking sheets, 1½ inches (4 cm) apart. Slightly flatten the tops and bake for 15 to 20 minutes. Let cool on the baking sheet 2 minutes before transferring to a rack to cool.

WHY USE ORGANIC ORANGE ZEST?
Don't use citrus peels unless they are organic. It is very difficult to avoid pesticide residue. The peel retains the many chemicals used in spraying. Many recipes require the zest, or the thin colored layer of peel, that contains flavorful citrus oils. You can remove the zest using a rasp, fine box grater, or zester.

CHOCOLATE MANGO MOUSSE

MAKES 6 TO 8 SERVINGS

1 large mango, diced
(1½ cups/350 mL)

1 medium avocado, diced
(¾ cup/180 mL)

¼ cup (60 mL) unsweetened
cocoa powder

2 tbsp (30 mL) ground
coffee beans

1 tsp (5 mL) vanilla extract

1 cup (250 mL) semisweet
chocolate chips, melted

When my daughter Mackenzie was a gymnast, this was her favorite snack after a practice. She said it was so satisfying, creamy, and not over-the-top sweet.

1. In a food processor, purée the mango, avocado, cocoa powder, coffee, and vanilla until smooth.

2. Melt the chocolate chips in a metal bowl set over a pan of simmering water.

3. Add the melted chocolate chips to the ingredients in the food processor and blend until smooth. Pour into small ramekins.

4. Chill for 15 minutes.

Chapter Four

FAIR TRADE
CHOCOLATE AND COCOA

FAIR TRADE
CHOCOLATE AND COCOA

Camino

Name of producer co-op:
Acopagro.

Location:
San Martin, Peru.

How did Camino connect with Acopagro?
Through partnership with Equal Exchange in the Co-operative Quality Development Program.

How many members are in the co-op?
8,000.

How many years have you been in business?
12.

How much food is grown in a season?
8,000 tons (7,257 metric tons) cocoa.

How is the crop harvested? Manually or with machines?
Cocoa pods are harvested by hand using pruners, then opened using a machete.

Where is it sold?
Switzerland, Netherlands, France, Germany, United States, Canada.

How have the farmers benefited from being a member of Fairtrade?
Fairtrade provided a market that allows an alternative to illicit crop growing, and taught quality standards that have allowed the co-op to earn an extra million dollars annually in the form of quality premiums.

What are your future plans?
We will bring more customers and investors to visit as we did in 2018.

Camino is owned by the La Siembra Co-operative in the Ottawa–Gatineau region of Canada. La Siembra means "sowing" or "planting time" in Spanish, a symbol for the seeds of change we are sowing through our cooperative and fair trade business models. La Siembra was established in 1999 by three young entrepreneurs. Having worked overseas, the founders of La Siembra experienced the exploitative nature of trade on the lives of family farmers. These three friends decided to provide Canadian consumers with an alternative to conventionally traded products by establishing a worker-owned cooperative.

Year one was spent in the community kitchen of First United Church, a socially progressive church in Ottawa. As there was no Fairtrade certification system for cocoa-based products at that time, La Siembra's founders adopted the guidelines of the Fairtrade Foundation. They began sourcing cocoa from a cooperative in Costa Rica and sugar from a mill supporting cooperative farmers in Paraguay. An organic recipe was developed, and the founders began to manufacture and distribute a hot chocolate, sugar, and cocoa line themselves. In 2002, La Siembra worked with Fairtrade Canada (then Transfair Canada) to develop a certification system for cocoa, chocolate, and sugar products in Canada, and became the first registered importers of Fairtrade-certified cocoa and sugar in North America.

CHOCOLATE

Why do people like chocolate so much? It is the third most valued ingredient after sugar and coffee. The complex flavor of chocolate is produced by 550 flavor compounds present in cocoa beans after they have been fermented, dried, and roasted. That's quite a large amount!

Always store chocolate in a cool, dry place. I never store chocolate around other household objects or foods that have a strong scent. Chocolate absorbs odors and will taste of those flavors if stored near them. My chocolate absorbed the scent of mint and oranges that were in my shopping bag. Be careful.

Chocolate is made from cacao beans, which grow on large tropical trees in Africa and Central and South America. The rainforest is the best environment for the cacao tree because it likes humidity and shade and the soil provides lush vegetation. They often grow 20 degrees north or south of the equator. There are three types of trees that produce cacao pods: Forastero, Criollo, and Trinitario.

The fruit of the cacao tree are oval-shaped pods as large as a footballs that grow out of the trunk. These can grow up to 15 inches (37 cm) and weigh up to 2 lbs (1 kg). When ripe, the pods can be red, green, or orange.

The botanical name for chocolate is Theobroma cacao, from the Ancient Greek for "food of the gods." Once the beans have been fermented and dried, we use the term cocoa.

Cocoa beans, like coffee beans, are bitter and never eaten raw. After they have been picked, the pods are cut open to reveal 40 to 45 beans surrounded by white pulp. They are placed in wooden boxes lined and covered with banana leaves and left for a week to ferment. Fermentation breaks down the sugars while other enzymes engage to produce chocolate flavors. The beans are then spread out in the sun for a week to harden and darken before they are ready to be shipped to the chocolate factory, where they are pitted and cleaned. The shells are forced open through a heavy press or mill to release the cocoa nibs, which are ground and roasted at 212°F (100°C). The heat from this process releases the beans' natural fat, called cocoa butter. Once removed, it leaves a dark paste called cocoa liquor. The paste will contain the flavor of chocolate.

To make chocolate, cocoa butter is added back to the cocoa liquor. (Better-quality chocolate only uses cocoa butter.) The paste of cocoa butter is combined with the cocoa liquor, then additional ingredients can be added. The amount of sugar, vanilla, milk solids, and spices can determine how sweet or aromatic chocolate tastes.

The next process, called conching, grinds, kneads, and aerates the chocolate. The smooth and glossy mixture requires three to four days to develop its flavor. When finished, the warm liquid chocolate is cooled and set into molds before being packaged. This process is called tempering.

Some chocolates are better for eating and some are better for cooking. Milk chocolate and sweet dark chocolate are usually eaten in a bar form. Darker chocolate with higher cocoa solids is best for baking; the flavor is too intense to eat raw.

Bittersweet chocolate with 70% cocoa solid content is best used in layer cakes, rich mousses, and flourless chocolate cakes. These desserts allow the flavor of chocolate to come through, as they don't require the addition of too much sugar.

Milk and white chocolate are very sweet and are best used for icings and ice cream. Semisweet chocolate is best used in glazes on cakes and in sauces. Frostings are best with this type of chocolate because it combines well with a small amount of sugar.

Unsweetened chocolate has an intense flavor and is usually mixed with large amounts of butter/oils and sweeteners. Brownies and cookies lend themselves well to this type of chocolate.

The terms cocoa liquor, cocoa solids, and cocoa mass are used on chocolate packaging.

NATURAL COCOA POWDER

When all the cocoa butter is removed from the cocoa liquor, it leaves a dry cake that is ground to a very fine powder. Bitter and acidic, it is best used in baked or cooked desserts.

I like to use natural cocoa powder for brownies, cakes, and cookies. It has a more intense flavor.

DUTCH PROCESS COCOA POWDER

This cocoa powder has a small amount of alkaline added to reduce the acidity and give it a more mellow flavor.

Dutch process cocoa is best used for icings, creams, and sauces. It has a more subtle, delicate flavor that will not overpower other tastes.

JALAPENO CHOCOLATE CHILI

MAKES 4 TO 6 SERVINGS

Chilies offer deep smoky and earthy flavors and are a base for many spicy sauces. They are a rich source of vitamin A. Jalapenos are large green chilies.

Unsweetened or bittersweet chocolate is a combination of cocoa solids and cocoa butter. It is too bitter to nibble but ideal for cooking, as its intense taste is not easily overpowered by competing flavors.

....

1. Slice the chili lengthwise; remove stem and seeds. To toast the chili, heat a small dry skillet over medium heat. Add the chili, pressing down with tongs for 1 minute, turn over, and toast for 30 seconds on the other side.

2. When cool, slice into 4 pieces. Pulse in a spice grinder until finely ground. Place in a small bowl with the cumin, oregano, cinnamon, and salt.

3. In a large saucepan, heat the olive oil over medium heat. Sauté the garlic for 1 minute. Add the onion and cook for 5 minutes or until softened. Add the mushrooms, corn, celery, spinach, and ½ cup (120 mL) water or stock. Cook covered and stir occasionally for 5 minutes.

4. Mix in the chili spice mixture. Stir in the chocolate and tomatoes. Reduce heat and simmer, covered, for 10 minutes.

5. Stir in the beans. Simmer for 5 more minutes or until the beans are hot.

6. Garnish each bowl with 2 tbsp (30 mL) cashews.

1 medium-size fresh jalapeno chili or 2 tsp (5 mL) chili powder

1½ tsp (7 mL) ground cumin

½ tsp (2 mL) dried oregano

¼ tsp (1 mL) ground cinnamon

1 tsp (5 mL) sea salt

2 tbsp (30 mL) extra virgin olive oil

2 tbsp (30 mL) finely chopped garlic

1 cup (250 mL) thinly sliced red onion

1 cup (250 mL) thinly sliced shiitake mushrooms

½ cup (120 mL) corn niblets, frozen or from a can

1 cup (250 mL) celery, cut into ½-inch (1 cm) pieces

1 lb (454 g) spinach, washed and thinly sliced

½ cup (120 mL) water or stock

1 oz/3 tbsp (28 g/45 mL) bittersweet chocolate, grated

One 28-oz (796 mL) can organic diced tomatoes

One 19-oz (540 mL) can organic pinto or white beans with liquid

½ cup (120 mL) toasted cashews

CHOCOLATE CHIP BARK

MAKES 1 LB (454 G)

2½ cups (600 mL) semisweet chocolate chips

¼ cup (60 mL) cocoa powder

3 tbsp (45 mL) coconut oil

2 tbsp (30 mL) crystallized ginger, finely chopped

½ cup (120 mL) dried cranberries

½ cup (120 mL) dried apricots, chopped

½ cup (120 mL) pecans, coarsely chopped

½ cup (120 mL) toasted sunflower seeds (see page 197)

½ cup (120 mL) dried pineapple, chopped

¼ cup (60 mL) dried unsweetened coconut

This is the perfect nibble. Use good-quality chocolate chips and organic dried fruit. So satisfying. My favorite going-on-a-car-trip snack. Store dried fruit in airtight containers away from light and heat.

1. In the top of a double boiler, or in a heatproof bowl set over a pan of hot water, place the chocolate chips, cocoa powder, oil, and ginger. Stir until the chocolate is melted. Remove from heat.

2. Add half of the cranberries, apricots, pecans, sunflower seeds, and pineapple. Mix well.

3. Spread the mixture evenly onto a rimmed baking sheet lined with parchment paper.

4. Sprinkle the top with the remaining cranberries, apricots, pecans, sunflower seeds, pineapple, and coconut.

5. Chill in the refrigerator for 30 minutes or until firm.

6. Break bark into bite-size pieces.

COCOA BARLEY SQUARES

MAKES 35 TO 40 PIECES

3 cups (700 mL) rolled oats

1 cup (250 mL) barley flakes

½ cup (120 mL) spelt flakes

¼ cup (60 mL) unsweetened cocoa powder

2 tbsp (30 mL) dried shredded coconut

1½ cups (350 mL) golden cane sugar

1 cup (250 mL) unsalted butter

2 tbsp (30 mL) maple syrup

1 tsp (5 mL) vanilla

Serve with your favorite beverage. Barley and spelt flakes are usually available in health food stores. Flakes are made from grains that are steam cooked, rolled into thin flakes, and sometimes toasted.

1. Preheat oven to 325°F (160°C).

2. In a large bowl, combine the oats, barley and spelt flakes, cocoa, and coconut.

3. Melt the sugar, butter, syrup, and vanilla in a medium-size saucepan. Stir until sugar dissolves—do not allow bubbles to form.

4. Pour the butter mixture over the oat mixture. Combine well.

5. Using a fork, press the mixture evenly into a lightly greased or parchment-lined rimmed baking sheet.

6. Bake for 20 minutes.

7. Allow to cool for 15 minutes. Slice into 35 to 40 pieces.

PISTACHIO POPCORN COOKIES

MAKES 30 COOKIES

Who doesn't enjoy popcorn? One day I had some leftover freshly popped popcorn, and my four-year-old son Emery said "I wish there were popcorn cookies to eat." I told him I would create a popcorn cookie recipe just for him. Use any nut—peanut, almond, or walnut. They all contribute a great texture and flavor. Grind the almonds in a spice grinder. Half a cup (120 mL) of almonds grinds into half a cup (120 mL) of almond powder.

....

1. Preheat oven to 350°F (180°C). Line 2 rimmed baking sheets with parchment paper.

2. In a large bowl, combine the bananas, oil, egg, and vanilla.

3. In a medium-size bowl, whisk together the oats, ground almonds, baking powder, cardamom, salt, and cinnamon.

4. Add the dry ingredients to the banana mixture and stir until combined.

5. Fold in the popcorn, chocolate chips, and pistachios.

6. Measure 1 heaping tablespoon (15 mL) and shape into a ball, pressing firmly with your hands. Place the balls 1 inch (2.5 cm) apart on the prepared baking sheet.

7. Bake for 15 to 17 minutes, rotating baking sheets from top to bottom once.

8. Remove from oven and allow cookies to cool on a wire rack for 10 minutes.

2 cups (480 mL) overly ripe mashed bananas (3 large)

¼ cup (60 mL) liquid coconut oil (heat if necessary)

1 large egg

1 tsp (5 mL) vanilla extract

1¼ cups (300 mL) rolled oats

½ cup (120 mL) ground almonds

1 tsp (5 mL) baking powder

½ tsp (2 mL) ground cardamom

½ tsp (2 mL) sea salt

¼ tsp (1 mL) ground cinnamon

2½ cups (600 mL) popped corn

1¼ cups (300 mL) semisweet chocolate chips

1 cup (250 mL) shelled pistachios, finely chopped

CHILI CHOCOLATE MUFFINS

MAKES 12 MUFFINS

2 tbsp (30 mL) minced fresh jalapeno chilies, red or green, finger-shaped

1½ cups (350 mL) all-purpose flour

½ cup (120 mL) unsweetened cocoa powder

1 tsp (5 mL) baking powder

½ tsp (2 mL) sea salt

½ cup (120 mL) light brown sugar

One 3½-oz (100 g) bar milk chocolate, coarsely grated

½ cup (120 mL) walnuts, thinly sliced

2 medium eggs

½ cup (120 mL) olive oil

1 cup (250 mL) coconut milk

1 tsp (5 mL) vanilla extract

Chili and chocolate complement each other so well. The heat from the chilies blends nicely with the creaminess of the milk chocolate and it's a great taste.

1. Preheat oven to 400°F (200°C). Line a 12-cup muffin pan with double-paper muffin cups.

2. Wearing rubber gloves, remove seeds and membranes from the chilies. Finely dice.

3. Mix the flour, cocoa, baking powder, and salt into a bowl. Stir in sugar, grated chocolate, and walnuts. Make a well in the center.

4. In a medium-size bowl, beat the eggs and oil until well-blended. Add the milk, vanilla, and jalapenos.

5. Pour the wet ingredients into the well and stir until just combined.

6. Spoon the mixture into the prepared muffin cups, filling each two-thirds full.

7. Bake for 20 minutes. Allow to cool for 10 minutes and place on a wire rack.

TIP: Fresh chilies contain volatile oils and you must not touch your eyes or mouth after handling one—they can sting and burn. Always wash your hands or wear gloves when handling fresh chilies.

FAIR TRADE • ÉQUITABLE
ORGANIC • BIOLOGIQUE

FREE OF PRIORITY
ALLERGENS

SANS ALLERGÈNES
PRIORITAIRES

cuisine
camino ®·MD
fair trade • équitable

Baking
Chocolate

Chocolat
à cuire

56%
CACAO
DE CACAO

Semi-Sweet ◎ Mi-sucré

200 g

Vous trouverez de savoureuses recettes sur notre site web ! camino.ca

cuisine
camino
fair trade • équit

Shred
Coco

Noix de

cuisine
camino

Baking
Chocolate
Chocolat
à cuire

Bittersweet ◎ Mi-amer

200 g

Vous trouverez de savoureuses recettes sur notre site web !
camino.ca

Bittersweet ◎ Mi

BITTERSWEET CHOCOLATE BROWNIES

MAKES 12 BROWNIES

When you combine good-quality cocoa powder with bittersweet chocolate, you have a depth of chocolate flavor that is remarkable. Moist and delicate, these brownies are the best!

....

1. Preheat oven to 375°F (190°C) and place rack in the middle. Butter and flour an 8-inch (20 cm) square cake pan.

2. Melt the chocolate and butter in a metal bowl set over a saucepan of simmering water. When melted, whisk until smooth.

3. Transfer the chocolate mixture to a medium-size bowl. Whisk in the sugar. Whisk in the eggs, one at a time, until well-combined. Stir in the vanilla.

4. In a small bowl, mix together the flour, cocoa, and salt. Add to the chocolate mixture. Whisk until combined.

5. Pour the batter into the baking pan and add pecans on top. Bake for 30 minutes.

6. Cool in the pan and cut into 12 pieces.

1 cup (250 mL) coarsely chopped bittersweet chocolate (5 oz/142 g)

½ cup (120 mL) unsalted butter at room temperature

¾ cup (180 mL) light brown sugar

3 large eggs

1 tsp (5 mL) vanilla extract

¼ cup (60 mL) all-purpose flour

¼ cup (60 mL) unsweetened cocoa powder

¼ tsp (1 mL) salt

1 cup (250 mL) pecans, coarsely chopped

MELTED CHOCOLATE CAKES

MAKES 6 SERVINGS

5 tbsp (75 mL) unsalted butter at room temperature, divided

10 oz (284 g) bittersweet chocolate, finely chopped

⅓ cup (80 mL) granulated sugar

2 large eggs

½ cup (120 mL) all-purpose flour

¼ tsp (1 mL) sea salt

My colorful ovenproof ceramic bowls are best known as ramekins. They are very versatile and can be used for hot dips, soups, or crème brulée. My brightly glazed ramekins are made in France by Emile Henry and are a welcome departure from the traditional white pots.

....

1. Preheat oven to 400°F (200°C). Brush the insides of six 6-oz/ ¾ cup (170 g/180 mL) ramekins with 1 tbsp (15 mL) melted butter between them.

2. Place the finely chopped chocolate in a heat-proof bowl set over a pan of simmering water. Stir until just melted.

3. Cream the remaining ¼ cup (60 mL) butter and sugar with an electric mixer until fluffy. Add the eggs one at a time, beating well after each addition.

4. On low speed, add the flour and salt. Add the chocolate. Mix until combined.

5. Divide the batter among the 6 prepared ramekins.

6. Place the ramekins on a rimmed parchment-paper-lined baking sheet for 12 minutes or until cakes are no longer shiny on top. Remove from oven, then remove from the baking sheet and let stand on a wire rack for 10 minutes.

7. When ready to serve, loosen the edges of the cakes and place on serving plates.

CHOCOLATE-DIPPED DRIED CHERRY BISCOTTI

MAKES 24 PIECES

Do you ever want a taste of chocolate that is bordered by a cookie? When you only dip one end of the biscotti in chocolate, you can still dip the other end of your biscotti in your coffee! You must wait until the biscotti are completely cooled before dipping them into the melted chocolate. It needs to be room temperature to coat—you wouldn't want to burn your fingers.

....

1. Heat oven to 350°F (180°C). Line a rimmed baking sheet with parchment paper

2. In a medium-size bowl, whisk together the flour, sugar, cinnamon, baking powder, baking soda, and salt.

3. In a small mixing bowl, whisk together the egg, egg yolk, orange zest, orange juice, and vanilla. Add the cherries.

4. Gently stir into the dry mixture until combined. Stir in the almonds.

5. With lightly floured hands, shape the dough into a 16- × 2-inch (40 × 5 cm) log and transfer to the parchment-lined baking sheet.

6. Bake in the oven for 25 minutes. Remove log to a cutting board and allow to cool for 10 minutes. Lower oven temperature to 325°F (160°C).

7. Using a serrated knife, cut the log crosswise into ½-inch (1 cm) pieces. Stand pieces on a baking sheet, leaving space between each.

8. Transfer the biscotti back to the previous baking sheet and bake an additional 15 minutes at 325°F (160°C).

9. Remove from oven and place on a wire rack to cool.

10. Line a rimmed baking sheet with a fresh piece of parchment paper.

11. Melt the chocolate in the top of a double boiler over hot water, stirring until melted. Remove pan from stove.

12. One at a time, dip one end of each biscotti into the chocolate, letting excess chocolate drip back into the pot, then place the biscotti on the parchment-lined baking sheet. Allow chocolate to cool and firm up for 20 minutes before eating.

1½ cups (350 mL) all-purpose flour

½ cup (120 mL) muscovado sugar

1 tsp (5 mL) ground cinnamon

½ tsp (2 mL) baking powder

¼ tsp (1 mL) baking soda

¼ tsp (1 mL) sea salt

1 large egg

1 egg yolk (from a large egg)

1 tbsp (15 mL) grated orange zest

2 tbsp (30 mL) orange juice

1 tsp (5 mL) vanilla extract

½ cup (120 mL) dried cherries

1 cup (250 mL) almonds, toasted and coarsely chopped

8 oz (227 g) bittersweet chocolate, chopped

GUINNESS COCOA CAKE

MAKES 12 SERVINGS

1 cup (250 mL) unsalted
butter at room temperature
+ extra for greasing

1½ cups (350 mL) packed
muscovado sugar

4 large eggs

1½ cups (350 mL) unbleached
white flour

1 cup (250 mL) unsweetened
cocoa powder

½ cup (120 mL) dried cranberries

2 tsp (10 mL) baking soda

½ tsp (2 mL) baking powder

1½ cups (350 mL) Guinness or
other stout beer

½ cup (120 mL) dark chocolate
(3 oz/85 g), finely grated

I have an old-fashioned box grater that has four sides for grating ingredients. I like to use the whole side because it grates easily and I never lose any skin off my fingers. My friend Raquel Fox, chef and caterer, uses beer in recipe development and encouraged me to use beer in a dessert. If you do not want to use beer in this recipe you can substitute soda water, same amount.

....

1. Preheat oven to 350°F (180°C). Line the bottom of a 9-inch (23 cm) springform pan with parchment paper. Grease the sides with butter. Line a rimmed baking sheet with foil. Set aside.

2. In a large bowl, using an electric mixer at medium speed, cream together the butter and sugar until light. Add the eggs one at a time, beating well after each addition.

3. In a small bowl, add the flour, cocoa, cranberries, baking soda, and baking powder. Mix well.

4. Add 1 cup (250 mL) of the flour mixture to the butter mixture, stir to combine, then add ¾ cup (180 mL) Guinness and stir. Continue adding flour and Guinness until they are used up. Mix well.

5. Pour the batter into the prepared springform pan. Bake on the foil-lined baking sheet for 1 hour 10 minutes. Cover cake with foil around the 50-minute mark if it browns too quickly.

6. Remove from oven and let stand for 8 to 10 minutes before removing from pan.

7. Sprinkle with chocolate. Let stand for 3 minutes.

TIP: When pouring beer, let the foam subside before mixing it into the batter.

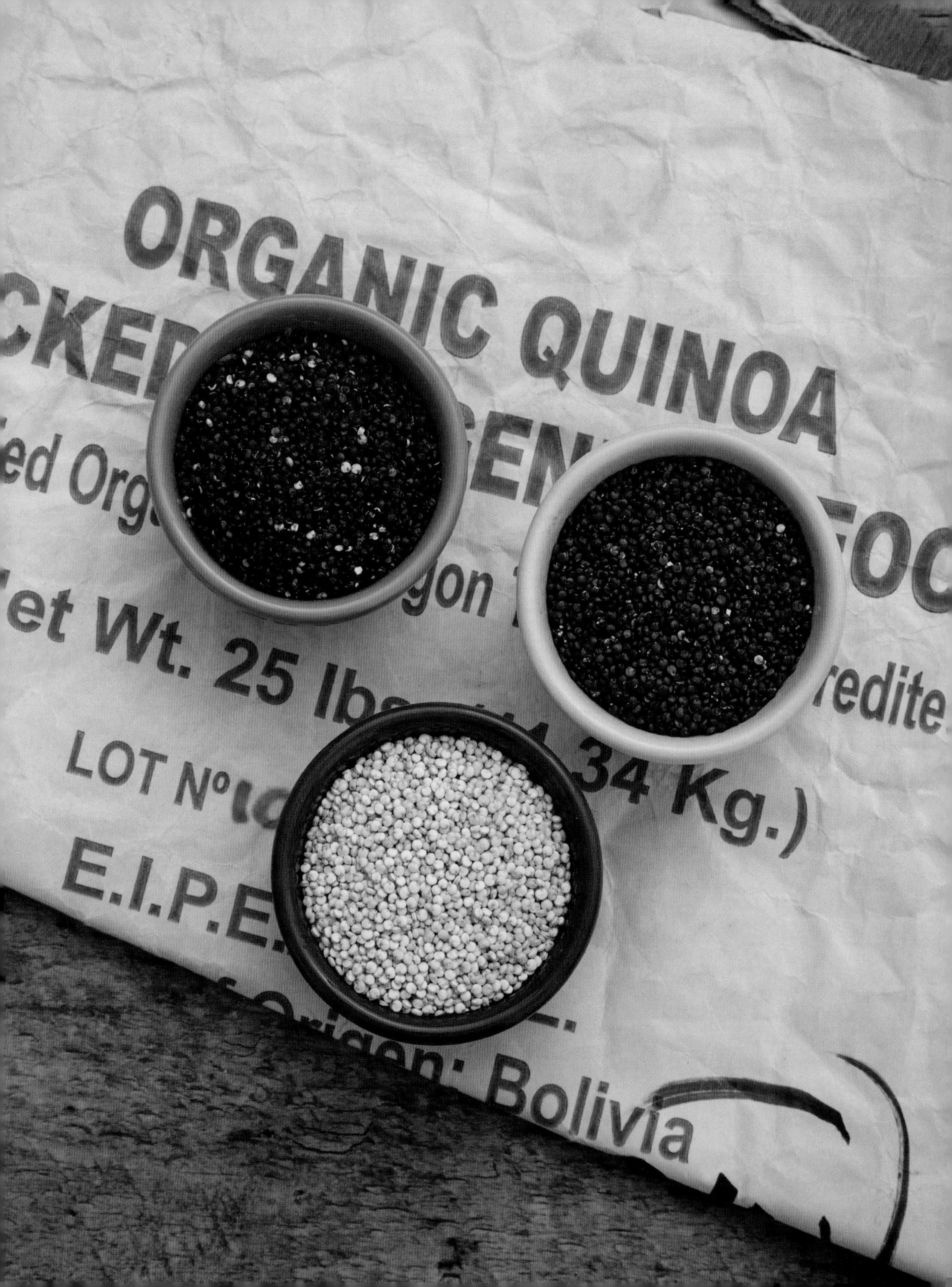
ORGANIC QUINOA
LOT N°
Bolivia

Chapter Five

FAIR TRADE
QUINOA

FAIR TRADE
QUINOA

Quinoa—Modern Day Superfood

Quinoa, known as the "mother of all grains," grows in the high valleys of the Andes Mountains. It grows best at 10,000 feet (3,050 meters), a high altitude. It can survive drought, hot sun, and frost well, and can grow in poor alkaline soil. It flourishes under extreme weather conditions.

Quinoa is a member of the Goosefoot family, and is the seed of a leafy green plant related to spinach. It was first documented 5,000 years ago and is referred to as an ancient grain. It is and was a staple of Incan civilization. It is a tiny disc-shaped grain. The periphery of each disk is bound with a narrow germ or embryo. While cooking, the wispy germ separates from the seed and the grain softens and absorbs its cooking liquid in 15 to 20 minutes, depending on the variety. Sold in tan, red, and black varieties, quinoa can be mixed and matched to provide a confetti-like assortment of colors. Quinoa is easy to digest.

The UN World Health Organization says quinoa is equal to milk in protein quality: 16%—the highest amount of complete protein in any grain. It contains calcium, iron, phosphorus, B vitamins, and vitamin E, zinc, potassium, riboflavin, and niacin. Unlike most grains (wheat, corn, barley), quinoa contains the key amino acid lysine in its proteins, and it contains all the amino acids needed for building muscles, tendons, and other tissues.

One cup (250 mL) of quinoa requires 2 cups (480 mL) liquid (water, orange juice, vegetable stock, coconut milk) to cook, and provides 3 cups (700 mL) cooked quinoa.

It is very important to rinse quinoa in a fine mesh strainer before cooking. Quinoa is covered in a bitter resin called saponin, which is a natural detergent that allows the grain to grow on its stalk without being eaten by insects or animals. When you rinse the quinoa, you will see tiny bubbles start to form at the base of your strainer. That is the saponin being rinsed away.

I often toast my quinoa after it has been rinsed. It retains its shape better, especially if it's going to be added to a stew after it has already absorbed cooking liquid.

You can buy quinoa pasta, flour, flakes, and cereal. I use quinoa flour as a thickener when preparing sauces.

QUINOA STEW WITH POTATOES, PEAS, AND CORN

MAKES 6 SERVINGS

Protein-packed quinoa with potatoes, corn, and avocado provides a hearty meal. Smoked paprika lends a subtle kick, and this really is a one-pot recipe. Use any type of rinsed quinoa; I prefer the tricolored for this recipe, as it adds to the presentation. My daughter Macko's boyfriend Ken suggests puréeing the soup for a thick, delicious texture.

....

1. Heat oil in a large pot over medium heat. Add the onion and garlic and cook, stirring frequently, for 5 to 7 minutes, or until softened and golden brown. Stir in the paprika, coriander, and cumin, and cook until combined, about 45 seconds.

2. Stir in the tomatoes, broth, and potatoes, and bring to a boil over high heat. Reduce heat to medium-low and simmer, covered, for 10 minutes.

3. Stir in the rinsed quinoa and simmer for 10 minutes. Add the corn and simmer for an additional 10 minutes. Stir in the peas and simmer until heated through, an additional 2 minutes.

4. Divide into 6 medium-size bowls and garnish with pumpkin seeds, avocado, and parsley.

2 tbsp (30 mL) olive oil

1 large Vidalia onion, chopped

4 large garlic cloves, minced

1 tbsp (15 mL) smoked paprika

2 tsp (10 mL) ground coriander

1 tsp (5 mL) ground cumin

One 28-oz (796 mL) can diced tomatoes

4 cups (950 mL) vegetable broth

1 lb (454 g) Yukon Gold mini potatoes, skin on, sliced in half

½ cup (120 mL) tricolored quinoa, rinsed

1 cup (250 mL) frozen peaches-and-cream corn

1 cup (250 mL) small frozen peas

½ cup (120 mL) toasted pumpkin seeds

1 large ripe avocado, pitted and diced

½ cup (120 mL) Italian parsley, finely chopped

ROASTED RED PEPPER SQUASH SALAD WITH QUINOA

MAKES 6 SERVINGS

2 cups (480 mL) vegetable stock

1 cup (250 mL) red quinoa, rinsed

2 cups (480 mL) peeled butternut squash, cut into ½-inch (1 cm) pieces

1 cup (250 mL) roasted red peppers, diced

¾ cup (180 mL) fresh cilantro, chopped

½ cup (120 mL) pistachios, shelled

1 tsp (5 mL) lime zest

¼ cup (60 mL) fresh lime juice

¼ cup (60 mL) olive oil

¼ tsp (1 mL) sea salt

⅛ tsp (0.5 mL) ground ginger

¾ cup (180 mL) chives, thinly sliced

This salad is terrific as a pita stuffer or ingredients for a wrap. The contrast in textures from creamy squash, crunchy pistachios, and chives will satisfy everyone and have people coming back for seconds.

....

1. Bring the stock to boil in a small pot. Add the rinsed quinoa. Reduce to a simmer, cover, and cook for 15 to 17 minutes. Set aside to cool.

2. Add enough water to reach the bottom of a collapsible steamer set in a saucepan and bring to a boil on high heat. Place the squash in the steamer basket, cover, and steam for 6 to 8 minutes. Remove the squash and set aside.

3. In a large bowl, combine the cooked quinoa, squash, roasted red peppers, cilantro, and pistachios.

4. In a small bowl, whisk together the zest, juice, oil, salt, and ginger.

5. Add dressing to the quinoa mixture. Add the chives. Toss to mix well.

TOASTED BLACK QUINOA
WITH SHALLOTS AND GOAT CHEESE

MAKES 4 TO 6 SERVINGS

How can you prevent your quinoa from ending up as a mushy mess? Toast the grains before cooking! Toasting develops quinoa's natural nuttiness, and it pairs so well with fresh herbs and crumbled goat cheese.

....

1. In a medium-size saucepan, toast the quinoa over medium-high heat, stirring frequently for 5 minutes. Quinoa will start to pop and needs to be stirred to toast evenly. Transfer to a small bowl.

2. Melt the butter in the same saucepan over medium heat. Add the shallots, garlic, and salt, and cook until the shallots are soft, about 3 to 5 minutes.

3. Stir in the stock and toasted quinoa, increase heat to medium-high, and bring to a boil. Cover, reduce heat to low, and simmer until the liquid is absorbed, 15 to 18 minutes, stirring once or twice.

4. Once all the stock has been absorbed, allow the mixture to sit, covered, for 5 minutes. Fluff quinoa with a fork.

5. Add the grated carrot, tomatoes, green onion, and lemon juice. Sprinkle with crumbled goat cheese before serving.

TIP: Spoon ½ cup (120 mL) salad onto a large leaf of romaine lettuce.

1 cup (250 mL) black quinoa, rinsed

3 tbsp (45 mL) salted butter

4 medium-size shallots, thinly sliced

3 medium-size cloves garlic, minced

½ tsp (2 mL) salt

2 cups (480 mL) vegetable stock

1 carrot, grated

½ cup (120 mL) sundried tomatoes, thinly sliced

3 tbsp (45 mL) green onions, chopped

2 tbsp (30 mL) lemon juice

½ cup (120 mL) crumbled goat cheese

SUNDRIED TOMATO CORNBREAD

MAKES 20 TO 24 PIECES

1½ cups (350 mL) quinoa flour

1¼ cups (300 mL) yellow cornmeal

½ cup (120 mL) packed brown sugar

1 tbsp (15 mL) baking powder

1 tsp (5 mL) sea salt

½ tsp (2 mL) baking soda

2½ cups (600 mL) buttermilk

3 large eggs

⅓ cup (80 mL) salted butter, melted

1 cup (250 mL) sundried tomatoes, chopped

½ cup (120 mL) fresh basil, finely chopped

¼ cup (60 mL) maple syrup

You can use roasted red peppers, pickled peppers, sweet Peruvian peppers, or any moist pickled pepper to flavor this cornbread made with quinoa flour. I always serve it warm, with a little drizzle of olive oil or a pat of butter. I like to eat it with Quinoa Parsnip Soup (see page 145).

1. Toast the quinoa flour in a medium-size skillet over medium heat, stirring constantly for about 5 minutes, or until golden. Let cool.

2. Preheat oven to 400°F (200°C). Grease a 13- × 9-inch (33 × 23 cm) baking pan.

3. In a large bowl, combine the flour, cornmeal, sugar, baking powder, salt, and baking soda.

4. In a medium-size bowl, whisk together the buttermilk, eggs, and butter until blended. Add the sundried tomatoes and basil. Mix well.

5. Add the buttermilk mixture to the flour mixture and stir just until mixed.

6. Pour the batter into the pan. Drizzle with maple syrup. Bake for 25 to 30 minutes, or until the edges are light brown.

TIP: To make your own buttermilk, add 1 tbsp (15 mL) white vinegar or fresh lemon juice to 1 cup (250 mL) milk. Stir and allow to stand for 5 minutes.

CHIPOTLE CHILI QUINOA WITH MIXED GREENS

MAKES 6 SERVINGS

This salad delivers quite a kick. You can increase the canned chili in adobo sauce for more heat. Combining avocado with toasted pumpkin seeds and tomatoes is a great way to contrast textures. The slight acidity of the tomatoes against the lush, smooth texture of the avocado makes the slight crunch of the pumpkin seeds all the more appealing. Toast that quinoa!

....

1. In a medium-size saucepan, toast the quinoa over medium heat for 5 minutes, stirring frequently. Quinoa will begin to pop and darken in color. Set aside.

2. Heat 2 tbsp (30 mL) olive oil in a saucepan over medium heat. Add leeks and cook until soft and lightly browned, 4 to 6 minutes.

3. Stir in the chipotle chili, tomato paste, and cumin and cook for 1 minute. Stir in the stock and toasted quinoa. Increase heat to medium-high, bring to a boil, and reduce heat to a simmer for 20 minutes. Cover and stir occasionally. Transfer to a bowl.

4. In a large bowl, whisk the remaining 2 tbsp (30 mL) olive oil, lime juice, salt, and pepper. Add the salad greens, chives, and cilantro. Toss to combine.

5. Add the chickpeas, tomatoes, and avocado. Toss to mix well.

6. Transfer to a serving platter and top with the quinoa mixture. Add pumpkin seeds.

½ cup (120 mL) red quinoa, rinsed

¼ cup (60 mL) olive oil, divided

2 cups (480 mL) sliced leeks, white and pale green parts only

1 tbsp (15 mL) canned chipotle chili in adobo sauce, finely chopped

1 tbsp (15 mL) tomato paste

1 tsp (5 mL) ground cumin

1 cup (250 mL) vegetable stock

¼ cup (60 mL) fresh lime juice

¼ tsp (1 mL) sea salt

⅛ tsp (0.5 mL) ground black pepper

One 5-oz (140 g) container of mixed salad greens

½ cup (120 mL) chives, thinly sliced

½ cup (120 mL) cilantro, chopped

One 14-oz (398 mL) can chickpeas, rinsed

2 cups (480 mL) cherry tomatoes, sliced in half

1 large ripe avocado, halved, pitted, and chopped

½ cup (120 mL) toasted pumpkin seeds (see page 197 Toasting Nuts and Seeds)

BREAKFAST QUINOA

MAKES 4 SERVINGS

1¾ cups (415 mL) coconut milk

¾ cup (180 mL) red quinoa, rinsed

1 tbsp (15 mL) maple syrup

½ tsp (2 mL) ground cinnamon

½ tsp (2 mL) vanilla extract

⅛ tsp (0.5 mL) sea salt

2 tbsp (30 mL) dried cherries or cranberries

2 tbsp (30 mL) currants or raisins

3 tbsp (45 mL) walnuts, chopped

2 tsp (10 mL) ground flax seeds

Easy to prepare ahead of time and reheat. I often add leftover bits of fresh fruit, too.

1. In a medium-size pot, bring the coconut milk to a boil. Add the quinoa. Return to a boil.

2. Add the maple syrup, cinnamon, vanilla, salt, cherries, and currants. Stir. Reduce heat to a simmer, cover, and cook for 15 minutes, or until the quinoa absorbs all the liquid.

3. Divide the mixture into 4 bowls and garnish with walnuts and ground flax seeds. Stir.

TOASTED SUNFLOWER–PUMPKIN SEED QUINOA CRUMBS

MAKES 3 CUPS (700 ML)

This is a perfect topping. I add it to salads, casseroles, cupcakes, and breakfast cereal.

....

1. Heat oven to 375°F (190°C). Line a rimmed baking sheet with parchment paper.

2. In a medium-size pot over high heat, bring the coconut milk to a boil. Add the quinoa and salt. Reduce heat to low, cover, and simmer for 20 to 25 minutes. Strain off any remaining milk in a fine mesh strainer.

3. In a large bowl, fluff the quinoa with a fork, breaking up any clumps. Add the sunflower and pumpkin seeds. Stir to combine.

4. In a small bowl, combine the cinnamon and nutmeg. Pour over the quinoa mixture. Stir well.

5. Spread the quinoa mixture on the prepared baking sheet. Drizzle with ¼ cup (60 mL) maple syrup. Bake for 25 minutes, stirring once. Use right away or cool and store in the fridge for a week.

2 cups (480 mL) water or coconut milk

½ cup (120 mL) red quinoa, rinsed

½ cup (120 mL) black quinoa, rinsed

¼ tsp (1 mL) sea salt

¼ cup (60 mL) sunflower seeds

¼ cup (60 mL) chopped pumpkin seeds

½ tsp (2 mL) ground cinnamon

½ tsp (2 mL) ground nutmeg

¼ cup (60 mL) maple syrup

QUINOA FALAFEL BALLS

MAKES TWENTY-FOUR 2-INCH (5 CM) BALLS

Baked or fried, these quinoa falafel balls are delicious. You can bake them and freeze them. They thaw quickly and can be used as a meatball in a spaghetti dish or as an appetizer, served with a Thai chili sauce. Stuffed in a pita or eaten on their own, they are easy to transport and taste great.

....

1. Preheat oven to 350°F (180°C). Line a rimmed baking sheet with parchment paper.

2. In a small pot, bring the stock to a boil. In a small skillet over medium heat, toast the quinoa for 5 minutes, stirring often. Add the toasted quinoa to the stock. Return to a boil. Lower heat to a simmer and cook for 15 minutes, or until the liquid has been absorbed.

3. In a large bowl, mix together the cooked quinoa, chickpeas, soy sauce, mirin, and garlic.

4. Stir in the chives, breadcrumbs, paprika, Parmesan cheese, and eggs.

5. Add the water or stock to the ground flax. Stir and wait 2 minutes for the mixture to thicken. Stir with a fork. Add to the quinoa mixture. Stir.

6. Form into twenty-four 2-inch (5 cm) balls. Bake in the oven for 20 to 25 minutes.

7. In a large skillet, heat 2 tbsp (30 mL) olive oil over medium heat, and brown 6 balls on all sides, 4 to 6 minutes. Use the remaining 2 tbsp (30 mL) olive oil for browning the additional 6 balls. Freeze the remaining 12 balls. (When you thaw them out, fry 6 at a time in 2 tbsp/ 30 mL olive oil, or bake in the oven at 350°F/180°C.)

8. Serve in a pita or on top of pasta.

*NOTE: The liquid in the chickpea can is called aquafaba (see page 152). It is an excellent vegan binding agent.

2 cups (480 mL) vegetable stock

1 cup (250 mL) tan or tricolored quinoa, rinsed

One 14-oz (398 mL) can chickpeas, drained (save the liquid*) and mashed (you can use a food processor)

2 tbsp (30 mL) soy sauce

1 tbsp (15 mL) mirin

4 garlic cloves, chopped

½ cup (120 mL) fresh chives, finely chopped

1 cup (250 mL) whole grain or panko breadcrumbs

2 tsp (10 mL) smoked paprika

1 cup (250 mL) freshly grated Parmesan cheese

2 large eggs, lightly beaten

2 tbsp (30 mL) flax seeds, ground

6 tbsp (90 mL) water, vegetable stock, or chickpea liquid

¼ cup (60 mL) olive oil, divided

QUINOA BOWL

MAKES 8 TO 10 SERVINGS

2½ cups (600 mL) vegetable stock, divided

1 cup (250 mL) tan quinoa, rinsed

1 tbsp (15 mL) olive oil

1 large Vidalia onion, thinly sliced

1 tbsp (15 mL) Dijon mustard

1 tbsp (15 mL) balsamic vinegar

1½ cups (350 mL) thinly sliced purple cabbage

1 cup (250 mL) grated carrot

1 cup (250 mL) frozen shelled edamame

Two 6-oz (170 mL) jars artichoke hearts, drained and coarsely chopped

2 tbsp (30 mL) toasted sunflower seeds (see page 197)

2 tbsp (30 mL) toasted pumpkin seeds (see page 197)

This is the perfect potluck recipe. Raw and marinated ingredients combine well to deliver that perfect bite. It is vegan, delicious, and plentiful.

1. In a medium-size pot, bring 2 cups (480 mL) stock to a boil. Add the quinoa. Reduce to a simmer, cover, and cook for 15 minutes. Remove from heat.

2. Heat the oil in a large skillet on medium heat. Add the onion. Cook until soft, 5 to 7 minutes, stirring often. Stir in the remaining stock, mustard, and balsamic vinegar. Bring to a simmer. Add the cabbage, carrot, and edamame. Cook for 5 minutes on low heat.

3. In a large bowl, toss the quinoa with the cabbage–carrot mixture. Add the artichoke hearts. Stir.

4. Garnish with sunflower and pumpkin seeds.

SHIITAKE MUSHROOM QUINOA OMELET WITH CHIVES

MAKES 4 SERVINGS

Have you ever cooked too much quinoa? This recipe is a perfect use for that leftover cup of cooked quinoa, fresh or frozen. Delicious hot or cold. My son Cameron would wolf a piece down after a hockey game, right out of the fridge.

....

1. In a small pot, bring the broth to a boil. Add the quinoa. Reduce to a simmer, cover, and cook for 15 minutes. Set aside.

2. In a medium-size skillet, heat the oil on medium heat. Add the shallot, salt, and pepper. Cook, stirring often, until light golden, 2 to 3 minutes.

3. Add the mushrooms. Cook until soft, 3 to 5 minutes.

4. In a small bowl, whisk together the eggs. Add the cooked quinoa.

5. Pour the egg mixture over the mushrooms. Cook, covered, for 5 to 7 minutes, or until the egg mixture is set.

6. Turn off the heat and sprinkle the omelet with cheese and chives. Cover. Let stand until the cheese has melted, about 2 to 3 minutes.

7. Cut into slices and serve.

1 cup (250 mL) vegetable broth

½ cup (120 mL) red quinoa, rinsed

1 tbsp (15 mL) olive oil

1 shallot, minced

¼ tsp (1 mL) sea salt

⅛ tsp (0.5 mL) ground black pepper

1 cup (250 mL) sliced shiitake mushrooms

4 large eggs

¼ cup (60 mL) shredded cheddar cheese

¼ cup (60 mL) chopped chives

BAKED QUINOA PUDDING WITH DRIED CHERRIES

MAKES 8 SERVINGS

3 cups (700 mL) soy or coconut milk, divided

1 cup (250 mL) tan quinoa, rinsed

¾ cup (180 mL) dried cherries, chopped

One 12.3-oz (350g) container silken tofu ¼ cup (60 mL) agave nectar

⅓ cup (80 mL) maple syrup + more for serving

1 tbsp (15 mL) vanilla extract

1 tsp (5 mL) ground cinnamon, divided

¼ cup (60 mL) brown sugar

½ tsp (2 mL) ground cardamom

My favorite way to bake this dessert is in individual ramekins. You can sprinkle the top of the pudding with fresh berries or add a teaspoon of maple syrup. My husband Jim likes to eat this for breakfast.

1. Position a rack in the middle of the oven and preheat to 375°F (190°C). Grease eight ¾-cup (180 mL) ramekins. Place on a rimmed baking sheet.

2. In a small pot, bring 2 cups (480 mL) soy milk to a boil. Add the quinoa. Reduce heat and simmer, covered, for 15 minutes, or until the liquid is absorbed.

3. Add the quinoa to a food processor. Pulse 3 times, 5 seconds each. Add the remaining soy milk and pulse until quinoa is creamy but not perfectly smooth. Pour the quinoa into a large bowl and return the food processor bowl to the base.

4. Using the food processor, add the tofu, agave nectar, maple syrup, vanilla, ½ tsp (2 mL) cinnamon, and process until smooth. Pour into the puréed quinoa and mix until combined.

5. Spoon into the prepared ramekins. Spray a piece of aluminum foil with cooking spray and place it on top of the ramekins. Bake for 15 minutes. Remove from oven and discard the foil.

6. Mix the sugar, remaining cinnamon, and cardamom in a small bowl. Sprinkle over the ramekins. Bake uncovered for 10 minutes longer, or until puddings are bubbling.

7. Remove from oven and cool on a wire rack for 10 minutes. Puddings will firm up as they cool.

OPTIONAL: Add 1 tsp (5 mL) maple syrup to each ramekin.

MARINATED TOFU CROUTONS WITH RED QUINOA STIR FRY

MAKES 6 SERVINGS

3 tbsp (45 mL) freshly squeezed
orange juice

2 tbsp (30 mL) freshly squeezed
lime juice

2 tbsp (30 mL) toasted sesame oil

½ inch (1 cm) fresh
ginger, minced

3 garlic cloves, minced

2 tsp (10 mL) white miso*

1 tsp (5 mL) rice vinegar

1 tsp (5 mL) soy sauce

1 tsp (5 mL) brown sugar

½ tsp (2 mL) ground black pepper

1 lb (454 g) extra firm tofu cut
into ½-inch (1 cm) pieces

2 cups (480 mL) vegetable stock

1 cup (250 mL) red quinoa, rinsed

¾ cup (180 mL) all-purpose flour

¾ cup (180 mL) dried
breadcrumbs

½ tsp (2 mL) sea salt

⅓ cup + 2 tbsp (110 mL)
olive oil, divided

4 medium-size shallots, chopped

1 red pepper, thinly sliced

8 cups (2 L) spinach, rinsed

1 tbsp (15 mL) fresh lemon juice

¼ cup (60 mL) toasted
pumpkin seeds

Crunchy citrus-marinated tofu is a real crowdpleaser. So moist and easy to prepare. Leftovers can be eaten for lunch the next day.

....

1. In a medium-size bowl, mix together the orange juice, lime juice, oil, ginger, garlic, miso, vinegar, soy sauce, sugar, and pepper. Set aside.

2. Cut the tofu into 1-inch (2.5 cm) pieces. Place in a medium-size glass bowl. Pour marinade over the tofu. Cover and marinate in the refrigerator for 45 minutes. Bring to room temperature.

3. In a medium-size pot, bring 2 cups (480 mL) stock to a boil. Add the quinoa. Reduce to a simmer, cover, and cook for 15 to 18 minutes. Remove from heat.

4. With a slotted spoon, lift the tofu croutons from the marinade and coat them with flour. Dip the croutons in the leftover marinade once more and coat with breadcrumbs. Set aside on a large plate.

5. In a large frying pan, heat ⅓ cup (80 mL) olive oil over medium heat. Fry the tofu, turning once until browned, about 2 minutes on each side. Set aside.

6. In a wok or large skillet, heat the remaining 2 tbsp (30 mL) olive oil over medium-high heat. Add the shallots and cook, stirring frequently, for 5 minutes or until soft and translucent.

7. Reduce heat to medium and add the red pepper. Stir for 2 minutes and add half the spinach. Stir for a minute and, as the spinach begins to shrink, add the remaining spinach along with 3 tbsp (45 mL) water to keep the spinach from sticking as it cooks. Cook, stirring and tossing, for 3 to 5 minutes until tender.

8. Add the quinoa and lemon juice and heat through.

9. Divide the spinach–quinoa mixture among 6 plates. Top each plate with tofu croutons. Garnish with pumpkin seeds.

*WHITE MISO: Miso is a fermented soybean and grain paste. White miso is high in rice and bacterial culture, but low in salt and it ferments quickly, usually in 8 weeks.

QUINOA CELERY SALAD WITH MISO DRESSING

MAKES 6 CUPS (1.5 L)

White miso paste is made from fermented soybeans and rice. It has a pale yellow color and a mild taste. Use it in place of soy sauce for a mild salty flavor. Lots of crunch in this recipe.

....

1. In a medium-size pot over high heat, bring the stock to a boil. Add quinoa, cover, reduce heat to a simmer, and cook for 18 minutes, or until all of the stock has been absorbed. Let stand for 5 minutes and fluff with a fork. Transfer the cooked quinoa to a large bowl.

2. In a medium-size mixing bowl, combine the miso, oil, vinegar, cilantro, mint, and honey. Whisk well. Pour on top of the quinoa. Stir to combine.

3. Add the shallot, celery, cucumber, carrot, tomatoes, and olives. Stir to combine.

4. Top with almonds.

2 cups (480 mL) vegetable stock

1 cup (250 mL) black quinoa, rinsed

2 tbsp (30 mL) white miso paste

2 tbsp (30 mL) toasted sesame oil

2 tbsp (30 mL) apple cider vinegar

3 tbsp (45 mL) cilantro, chopped

3 tbsp (45 mL) fresh mint, chopped

1 tbsp (15 mL) honey

1 shallot, finely chopped

2 celery ribs, diagonally sliced

Half an English cucumber, diced

1 carrot, grated

14 grape tomatoes, halved

½ cup (120 mL) pitted small green olives

½ cup (120 mL) tamari-roasted almonds, chopped

QUINOA SALMON BAKE

MAKES 4 TO 6 SERVINGS

2 cups (480 mL) vegetable stock

1 cup (250 mL) tan quinoa, rinsed

3 tbsp (45 mL) tomato paste

½ cup (120 mL) basil, chopped

2 tbsp (30 mL) olive oil

1 large Vidalia onion, diced

2 garlic cloves, minced

1 cup (250 mL) mixed
mushrooms, diced

1 cup (250 mL) diced zucchini

2 stalks celery, diced

1 cup (250 mL) roasted red
peppers, thinly sliced

One 6-oz (170 g) can wild pacific
pink salmon, drained

½ cup (120 mL) frozen
corn, thawed

¼ tsp (1 mL) sea salt

¼ cup (60 mL) salted butter

½ cup (120 mL) quinoa flour

1½ cups (350 mL) 2% milk or
plain soy milk

2 cups (480 mL) grated cheddar
cheese, divided

½ tsp (2 mL) sea salt

¼ tsp (1 mL) paprika

Buying sustainable salmon products is a great way to support the conservation of fish stocks. We need to read our labels and ensure our spending dollars are supporting the best practices. This is such an elegant casserole. My husband Jim likes to eat the leftovers in a warm pita.

....

1. Preheat oven to 350°F (180°C). Grease a 9- × 13-inch (23 × 33 cm) Pyrex dish or pan.

2. In a medium-size pot, bring the stock to a boil. Add the quinoa. Cover, reduce to a simmer, and cook for 15 minutes. Remove from heat and fluff with a fork.

3. Transfer to a large bowl and stir in the tomato paste and basil.

4. In a large saucepan, heat the oil and sauté the onion for 3 to 5 minutes until soft. Add the garlic, mushrooms, zucchini, celery, and peppers. Cook for 8 minutes. Add the salmon, corn, and salt. Stir to combine. Set aside.

5. To make the sauce, melt the butter in a medium-size saucepan over medium heat. Whisk in the quinoa flour and cook, whisking constantly, for 2 minutes, or until thickened. Gradually whisk in the milk. Cook, whisking constantly, for 3 to 5 minutes, or until thickened. Stir in 1 cup (250 mL) cheese, salt, and paprika. Cook, stirring constantly, for 2 minutes, or until the cheese is melted. Remove from heat.

6. Cover the bottom of the prepared pan with the quinoa mixture. Top with the sautéed vegetable–salmon mixture.

7. Spread the sauce smoothly over the top. Sprinkle the remaining cheese over the sauce.

8. Bake for 20 to 25 minutes. Let cool slightly before serving.

QUINOA LENTIL BURGERS WITH AQUAFABA

MAKES 6 SERVINGS

1½ cups (350 mL) water

½ cup (120 mL) black lentils

1 cup (250 mL) vegetable stock

½ cup (120 mL) red quinoa, rinsed

5 tbsp (75 mL) olive oil, divided

1 large Vidalia onion, chopped

3 large garlic cloves, minced

2 cups (480 mL) assorted mushrooms, trimmed and thinly sliced

1 tsp (5 mL) soy sauce

1 celery rib, minced

½ cup (120 mL) tamari-roasted almonds, ground

⅓ cup (80 mL) aquafaba (see page 152)

1 cup (250 mL) panko breadcrumbs

1 cup (250 mL) parsley, chopped

1 tsp (5 mL) sea salt

Sliced tomatoes, avocado slices, and bread and butter pickles for garnish

A vegan veggie burger that delivers flavor and fiber. Lentils contribute an earthiness that goes well with quinoa's texture. Mushrooms, almonds, and garlic add a savory richness that complements the dish. An introduction to aquafaba, the starchy liquid in a can of chickpeas, will be the best binding agent you have ever used in a burger. Move over eggs!

1. Heat oven to 300°F (150°C) and place rack in the middle position. Line a rimmed baking sheet with parchment paper.

2. In a small pot, bring the water to a boil. Add the lentils. Reduce heat to a simmer and cook the lentils for 20 minutes. Drain well.

3. In a small pot, bring the stock to a boil. Add the quinoa, reduce heat to low, cover, and simmer for 15 minutes. Strain off any remaining water in a fine mesh strainer.

4. Heat 2 tbsp (30 mL) oil in a medium-size skillet over medium heat. Add the onion and sauté for 3 to 5 minutes or until soft. Add the garlic. Sauté for 1 minute and add the mushrooms, soy sauce, and celery. Cook for 10 to 15 minutes. Drain any residual liquid.

5. Combine the lentils, quinoa, onion–vegetable mixture, ground almonds, and aquafaba in a food processor. Coarsely grind for 10 to 12 pulses.

6. Transfer the mixture to a large bowl. Stir in the panko, parsley, and salt.

7. Divide the mixture into 6 equal portions and pack into four 1-inch (2.5 cm) wide patties. Place on the baking sheet. Bake for 20 minutes.

8. In a large skillet, heat 2 tbsp (30 mL) oil over medium heat. Lay 4 patties in the pan and cook until crisp and browned on the first side, about 3 minutes. Gently flip the patties and cook until crisp and brown on the other side. Add an extra 1 tbsp (15 mL) oil if the pan is dry.

TIP: Patties can be served after being baked in the oven; there's no need to fry them in oil if you prefer not to.

QUINOA PARMESAN RISOTTO

MAKES 4 TO 6 SERVINGS

½ cup (120 mL) dried mushrooms

¼ cup (60 mL) salted butter

1 leek, chopped

1 cup (250 mL) thinly sliced fresh shiitake mushrooms

1¼ cups (300 mL) tan quinoa, rinsed

¼ tsp (1 mL) sea salt

⅛ tsp (0.5 mL) ground black pepper

½ cup (120 mL) dry white wine

2½ cups (600 mL) vegetable stock

½ cup (120 mL) freshly grated Parmesan

½ cup (120 mL) crumbled Gorgonzola

¼ cup (60 mL) parsley, chopped

I have done the unthinkable—I've removed Arborio rice, replaced it with quinoa, and called my recipe a risotto! To me, risotto is all about layering flavors, and the use of fresh and dried mushrooms, leeks, and wine all contribute to a simple yet luxurious meal.

1. Place dried mushrooms in a medium-size bowl. Cover with 1½ cups (350 mL) boiling water and set aside until softened, 8 to 10 minutes. Strain and reserve the soaking liquid, discarding any sediment. Chop the mushrooms, discarding any tough stems.

2. Heat the butter in a large skillet over medium heat. Add the leek, dried mushrooms, and fresh mushrooms. Cook, stirring occasionally, until the leeks begin to brown, about 5 minutes.

3. Add the quinoa and stir until glossy and coated with butter. Add the salt and pepper. Add the wine. Stir. When the liquid has been absorbed, add the mushroom soaking liquid. Lower heat to simmer.

4. When the liquid has been absorbed, add ½ cup (120 mL) stock and stir. Continue to add ½-cup (120 mL) amounts of stock until all the stock has been used up. Stir the risotto with each addition of stock.

5. Taste the mixture when all the stock has been absorbed, around 20 minutes. Quinoa should be tender but not mushy. Add cheeses and stir until they melt. Garnish with parsley.

QUINOA PARSNIP SOUP

MAKES 6 SERVINGS

The tart taste of the green apple adds a level of flavor that balances the sweetness of the parsnips and highlights the creamy texture of the quinoa.

....

1. In a large pot, heat the oil over medium heat. Cook the leeks and onion for 5 minutes or until softened. Stir. Add the celery, apple, and parsnips. Add the stock. Cook for 5 minutes.

2. Add the quinoa, tomato purée, and rosemary. Bring to a boil. Reduce heat and simmer for 15 to 18 minutes.

3. Transfer in batches to a food processor or blender. Process until smooth.

4. Return to the pot over medium heat. Add salt and pepper. Stir.

5. Serve, garnished with basil.

2 tbsp (30 mL) olive oil

2 large leeks (white part only), rinsed and thinly sliced

1 medium red onion, thinly sliced

3 stalks celery, thinly sliced

1 green apple, unpeeled, cut into 1-inch (2.5 cm) pieces

2 medium-size parsnips, rinsed and sliced into 1-inch (2.5 cm) rounds

6 cups (1.5 L) vegetable stock or water

1 cup (250 mL) tan quinoa, rinsed

One 28-oz (796 mL) can tomato purée or diced tomatoes

1 tsp (5 mL) crushed dried rosemary

1 tsp (5 mL) sea salt

½ tsp (2 mL) black pepper

2 tbsp (30 mL) fresh basil, chopped

Chapter Six

FAIR TRADE
SUGAR

FAIR TRADE
SUGAR

Camino

MUSCOVADO BROWN SUGAR

Name of producer co-op:
Co-op Norandino.

Location:
Piura, Peru.

How did Camino connect with Co-op Norandino?
Through the network of fair trade co-ops. When they launched the sugar
project, we made the connection.

How many members are in the co-op?
4,000.

How many years have you been in business?
20.

How much food is grown in a season?
8,000 tons (7,257 metric tons) coffee, 2,000 tons (1,814 metric tons) cocoa,
2,000 tons (1,814 metric tons) muscovado.

How is the crop harvested? Manually or with machines?
Manually with machetes. Artisanal processing of sugar cane to muscovado.

Where is it sold?
Italy, Canada, and France.

How have the farmers benefited from being a member of Fairtrade?
Gained customers and learned about quality control from fair trade buyers.

What are your future plans?
Use the cocoa liquor from their new factory to make chocolate in Canada.

GOLDEN SUGAR

Name of producer co-op:
Manduva.

Location:
Ahorros y Estrenos, Paraguay.

How did Camino connect with Manduva?
Camino was a pioneer in sugar; we sought out the farmer co-op as they
were forming.

How many members are in the co-op?
4,000.

How many years have you been in business?
20.

How much food is grown in a season?
20,000 tons (18,144 metric tons).

How is the crop harvested? Manually or with machines?
Manually cut, transported by truck, but sometimes by ox cart.

Where is it sold?
Canada, Netherlands, England, and Switzerland.

How have the farmers benefited from being a member of Fairtrade?
Exploited farm workers organized and found fair trade buyers to break
control by political elites, so they could export their own crops.

What are your future plans?
We have ensured only their sugar is used in making our chocolates.

Aquafaba

From the Latin aqua (water) and faba (bean), aquafaba is the leftover liquid in a can of chickpeas. During the cooking process, natural nutrients in the legumes are transferred to the water. There is 90% water to 10% protein and starch. This is the same ratio found in chicken egg whites. The similarity of these two liquids allows us to substitute aquafaba for egg whites in dessert recipes. It is a very good binder. You can whip it and create foam. In baking terms, it traps air, giving your baked goods structure and a fluffy crumb. Unlike eggs, however, there is no protein in aquafaba.

Neutral in taste and color, it can be used in sweet and savory recipes. Start experimenting. Three tbsp (45 mL) aquafaba equals 1 whole egg, and 2 tbsp (30 mL) aquafaba equals 1 egg white.

When buying chickpeas in a can, keep an eye out for brands that add unnecessary ingredients or additives. Choose canned beans carefully and ensure that the cans do not contain bisphenol A (BPA) in the can lining. An industrial chemical, BPA is used to make the epoxy resin that lines cans and can migrate into the beans. Look for BPA-free alternatives.

It is very important to shake the unopened chickpea can first. The starches in the chickpea liquid settle at the bottom of the can. You want them evenly distributed through the liquid to obtain the best quality aquafaba.

Drain the chickpeas through a fine mesh strainer over a larger bowl. Whisk the aquafaba liquid to distribute the starches and then measure. If you are not going to use the chickpeas, you can freeze them in a bag or ice cube tray. I fill the ice cube tray with 3 tbsp (45 mL) chickpeas and add 2 tbsp (30 mL) water to each individual cube.

Fresh aquafaba will last in the fridge for 1 week. Keep it in a tightly sealed glass jar or bottle. It may have a cloudy liquid at the bottom with a clear liquid rising in the middle section. No worries. This is normal. Shake the jar contents gently and they will merge.

I like to freeze aquafaba in 1- and 2-tbsp (15 and 30 mL) amounts in an ice cube tray. Once they have frozen, you can place the cubes in a plastic bag. I have had lots of success with thawed aquafaba. It whips up just as well as if fresh from the can.

In sweet recipes, sugar is added as a stabilizing ingredient. You will need to heat the aquafaba, dissolve the sugar in it, then whip the mixture to obtain stiff peaks. Another ingredient that adds to the stability of the whipped aquafaba is cream of tartar, which is acidic. Often added to egg whites, it creates foam that traps air bubbles and water more quickly and holds them

in place. Combining sugar and cream of tartar requires 5 minutes to reach a stiff foam, instead of 10 minutes without cream of tartar.

Use a stand mixer, electric whisk, or hand blender to turn your aquafaba into soft peaks. When using a stand mixer, you need to use ⅓ cup (80 mL) aquafaba in order to obtain peaks.

ORGANIC MERINGUES MADE WITH AQUAFABA

MAKES 40 MERINGUES

Move over egg whites, this is the perfect vegan substitute ingredient. Make sure your sugar is vegan as well. Most white sugar is filtered through animal bone char to bleach it. Camino has the best organic fair trade vegan sugar on the market.

....

1. Preheat oven to 225°F (110°C). Adjust oven racks to upper and lower middle positions. Line 2 rimmed baking sheets with parchment paper.

2. In a small pot over medium heat, add the sugar and aquafaba and whisk until the sugar is completely dissolved, 3 to 5 minutes. Mixture should not bubble. Cool the mixture then whisk in the cornstarch.

3. Using a stand mixer with the whisk attachment, whip the aquafaba mixture, almond extract, cream of tartar, and salt on high speed for 12 to 14 minutes, until stiff peaks form. It will be very sticky.

4. Place the meringue in a pastry bag fitted with a ½-inch (1 cm) plain tip. Pipe meringues into 1-inch (2.5 cm) wide mounds with 1-inch (2.5 cm) heights on baking sheets.

5. Bake for 2 hours, rotating sheets halfway. Turn off the oven and let meringues cool inside for 1 hour, or until dry and crisp. Remove from oven and cool before serving.

6. Store between wax or parchment paper in a cookie tin at room temperature for 1 week.

¾ cup (180 mL) organic granulated white sugar

½ cup (120 mL) aquafaba (see page 152)

2 tsp (10 mL) cornstarch

¼ tsp (1 mL) almond extract

¼ tsp (1 mL) cream of tartar

⅛ tsp (0.5 mL) sea salt

BROWNIE COOKIES

MAKES 24 COOKIES

7 oz (200 g) bittersweet chocolate, finely chopped

⅓ cup (80 mL) all-purpose flour

¼ tsp (1 mL) baking powder

¼ tsp (1 mL) salt

¼ cup (60 mL) unsalted butter at room temperature

⅓ cup (80 mL) granulated sugar

⅓ cup (80 mL) golden sugar

2 large eggs

¾ tsp (4 mL) vanilla extract

½ cup (120 mL) pecans, finely chopped

Who said a brownie cannot be a cookie? There are times when I want a hit of intense chocolate and one of these cookies fulfills that desire.

1. Preheat oven to 350°F (180°C). Line 2 rimmed baking sheets with parchment paper.

2. Place the chocolate in a bowl that fits over a pot of hot water. Stir until melted, then remove the bowl from the pot and let cool.

3. In a small bowl, whisk together the flour, baking powder, and salt.

4. In a large bowl, using an electric mixer, beat the butter and both sugars on medium-high speed until fluffy.

5. Add the eggs and vanilla. Beat until combined.

6. With the mixer on low speed, add the chocolate and flour mixture in alternating batches.

7. Mix until just combined. Fold in the chopped pecans.

8. Drop the dough 1 tbsp (15 mL) at a time, placing cookies 2 inches (5 cm) apart on the baking sheets.

9. Bake, rotating the sheets after 7 minutes. Cookies will bake for 13 to 15 minutes. Insert a toothpick in the center of a cookie to check for doneness.

10. Transfer cookies to a wire rack to cool.

PEANUT BUTTER CHOCOLATE CHIP COOKIES

MAKES 40 TO 45 COOKIES

This is a perfect cookie for your bake sale or cookie exchange. You can also use a ¼ cup (60 mL) measurement to make larger cookies, or use the batter to make 20 small and 12 large cookies. Almond nut or pumpkin seed butter can be used instead of peanut butter.

....

1. Heat oven to 325°F (160°C). Line 2 rimmed baking sheets with parchment paper. Set aside.

2. In a small bowl, whisk the flour, baking soda, and salt.

3. In a large bowl with a mixer on medium-high speed, beat the butter, peanut butter, and sugars until well-combined. Beat in the eggs and vanilla until blended.

4. Stir in the flour mixture until absorbed and a dough forms. Add the chocolate chips and almonds. Mix well.

5. Using a 1-tbsp (15 mL) measure, drop the dough in slightly rounded mounds onto the prepared baking sheets, spacing 2 inches (5 cm) apart.

6. Bake for 20 minutes or until golden brown around the edges. Cool cookies on the baking sheets on wire racks for 5 minutes. Transfer cookies to plates to cool completely.

2¼ cups (530 mL) all-purpose flour

1 tsp (5 mL) baking soda

1 tsp (5 mL) sea salt

1 cup (250 mL) unsalted butter at room temperature (2 sticks)

1 cup (250 mL) creamy peanut butter

1 cup (250 mL) golden sugar

½ cup (120 mL) granulated sugar

2 large eggs

1 tsp (5 mL) vanilla extract

8 oz (227 g) semisweet chocolate chips

1 cup (250 mL) coarsely chopped almonds

DARK ROAST CHOCOLATE CAKE

MAKES 24 PIECES

CAKE

5 oz/10 tbsp (142 g/150 mL) unsalted butter at room temperature

2 cups (480 mL) all-purpose flour

5 tbsp (75 mL) unsweetened cocoa powder

2 tsp (10 mL) baking powder

½ tsp (2 mL) sea salt

2 large eggs

1 cup (250 mL) muscovado brown sugar

¾ cup (180 mL) coconut milk

1 tsp (5 mL) vanilla extract

GANACHE

3 tbsp (45 mL) ground espresso coffee beans

½ cup (120 mL) 35% whipping cream

5oz (142g) bittersweet dark chocolate, finely chopped in a medium-size bowl

2 tbsp (30 mL) unsalted butter at room temperature

1 cup (250 mL) chopped almonds

Who doesn't adore dark chocolate and strong coffee? This is a perfect mid-afternoon snack when you feel peckish, and it always motivates me to finish the chore at hand.

CAKE

1. Preheat oven to 375°F (190°C). Grease and flour a 9- × 13-inch (23 × 33 cm) baking pan.

2. In a small saucepan, melt the butter. Remove from heat. Set aside.

3. In a medium-size bowl, stir together the flour, cocoa powder, baking powder, and salt.

4. In a large bowl, whisk the eggs with the sugar until frothy. Add the milk, melted butter, and vanilla. Whisk until blended.

5. Add the flour mixture and stir until you have a smooth batter. Pour into the prepared baking pan.

6. Bake for 14 to 16 minutes. Remove from the oven and place on a wire rack. Let cool in the pan for 10 minutes. Transfer cake to a rack and cool completely.

GANACHE

7. To make the ganache, boil 1 cup (250 mL) water in a pot or kettle. Place a coffee filter (size #2) in a 1-cup (250 mL) filter holder and spoon coffee into the filter. Place over a small tea or coffee cup. Pour ½ cup (120 mL) boiling water over the ground coffee. Measure 3 tbsp (45 mL) coffee and add to the cream in a small saucepan.

8. Over medium heat, bring the cream and coffee to a boil, 3 to 5 minutes.

9. Pour over the chocolate in the bowl. Whisk until the chocolate is melted. Add the butter and stir until combined. Allow to cool for 30 minutes.

10. Spread the ganache over the cake and top with chopped nuts. Cut into 24 pieces. This cake freezes well.

CHOCOLATE CHIP SUGAR COOKIES

MAKES 24 COOKIES

Mini chocolate chips are so popular. I really like to use them in a cookie recipe where a 1-tbsp (15 mL) measurement is used. The amount of chocolate chips is just right. The cloves and nutmeg add a sweet-spicy aroma.

··

1. Preheat oven to 375°F (190°C). Line 2 rimmed baking sheets with parchment paper.

2. In a medium-size bowl, mix the oats, flour, salt, baking soda, cinnamon, cloves, and nutmeg.

3. In a large bowl, using a handheld mixer, cream the butter and sugar together; mix in the egg and vanilla.

4. Add the dry ingredients to the butter mixture, blending well.

5. Stir in the chocolate chips, currants, and coconut.

6. Drop by rounded tablespoonfuls onto the prepared sheets. Bake for 8 to 10 minutes. Let cool on baking sheets for 2 minutes. Transfer cookies to a rack to cool.

1½ cups (350 mL) small oats

¾ cup (180 mL) unbleached white flour

½ tsp (2 mL) sea salt

½ tsp (2 mL) baking soda

½ tsp (2 mL) ground cinnamon

¼ tsp (1 mL) ground cloves

¼ tsp (1 mL) ground nutmeg

½ cup (120 mL) unsalted butter at room temperature

1 cup (250 mL) brown muscovado sugar

1 large egg

½ tsp (2 mL) vanilla extract

¾ cup (180 mL) mini chocolate chips

½ cup (120 mL) currants

¼ cup (60 mL) flaked coconut, unsweetened

MUSCOVADO SUGAR WALNUT CAKE

MAKES 8 TO 10 SERVINGS

TOPPING

1 medium-size orange

1 small lemon

1 cup (250 mL) water

½ cup (120 mL) brown sugar

¼ cup (60 mL) maple syrup

½ cup (120 mL) toasted walnuts, coarsely chopped

¼ cup (60 mL) dried cherries, chopped

CAKE

⅓ cup (80 mL) extra virgin olive oil, divided

1 cup (250 mL) toasted walnuts

½ cup (120 mL) full-fat yogurt

2 large eggs

¾ cup (180 mL) packed muscovado brown sugar

1 tsp (5 mL) vanilla

1 cup (250 mL) all-purpose flour

½ tsp (2 mL) baking powder

½ tsp (2 mL) baking soda

½ tsp (2 mL) ground cardamom

¼ tsp (1 mL) sea salt

Can a cake be made with olive oil and not a teaspoon of butter and still be delicious? The answer is yes.

....

1. Preheat oven to 350°F (180°C).

TOPPING

2. Cut the orange and lemon into ½-inch (1 cm) pieces. Remove any seeds. In a medium-size saucepan, combine the orange, lemon, water, sugar, and maple syrup. Bring to a boil over high heat, stirring often, then lower heat to a simmer and cook for 35 minutes or until the fruit is soft. Transfer to a food processor and pulse until the mixture is thick. Transfer to a small bowl.

CAKE

3. Using 2 tsp (10 mL) olive oil, oil the bottom and sides of a 9-inch (23 cm) cake pan. You can use a piece of parchment paper cut to fit the bottom of the pan. Oil it as well.

4. In a food processor, pulse 1 cup (250 mL) walnuts until finely ground.

5. In the bowl of a stand mixer, combine the yogurt, eggs, sugar, remaining olive oil, and vanilla. Mix at medium speed until combined.

6. In a medium-size bowl, combine the flour, baking powder, baking soda, cardamom, and salt. Add to the olive oil mixture. Mix until well-combined. Add the ground walnuts and mix until combined.

7. Pour the batter into the prepared cake pan and bake 30 to 35 minutes. Let the cake cool and invert onto a wire rack. Remove pan and cool before adding the topping.

8. Spread the orange–lemon mixture evenly over the top of the cake. Garnish with chopped walnuts and cherries.

CRANBERRY RICOTTA QUINOA SQUARES

MAKES 24 SQUARES

1¼ cups (300 mL) quinoa flour

1 cup (250 mL) bittersweet chocolate chips

1 cup (250 mL) salted butter

1 cup (250 mL) cranberry juice (blend is fine)

1 cup (250 mL) dried cranberries

½ cup (120 mL) packed brown sugar

2 large eggs

1 tsp (5 mL) vanilla extract

½ cup (120 mL) full-fat yogurt

1½ cups (350 mL) crumbled ricotta cheese

1 tbsp (15 mL) icing sugar

This is my cheesecake equivalent. Moist, creamy, and sweet. Camino has mini chocolate chips that work just as well.

....

1. Preheat oven to 325°F (160°C). Grease a 9-inch (23 cm) square cake pan.

2. Toast the flour in a medium-size skillet over medium heat, stirring for about 5 minutes, or until golden brown. Allow to cool.

3. In a medium-size saucepan on medium heat, melt the chocolate chips and butter, stirring often. When smooth, set aside to cool.

4. In a small saucepan, bring the cranberry juice to a boil. Place cranberries in a small bowl. Pour the hot cranberry juice over the cranberries. Let stand for 5 minutes. Drain, discarding the cranberry juice.

5. In a medium-size bowl, beat the sugar, eggs, and vanilla until combined. Stir in the melted chocolate–butter mixture until well-combined.

6. Mix in the flour until just combined, then add the yogurt and stir well.

7. Spread half the batter into the prepared pan. Sprinkle half the cranberries and drop ricotta cheese by spoonfuls over top of the batter, spreading the ricotta evenly.

8. Spoon the other half of the batter on top and carefully spread it evenly. Sprinkle with the remaining cranberries.

9. Bake for 40 to 45 minutes. Cool in the pan on a rack. Dust with icing sugar before serving.

PUMPKIN SEED BUTTER FUDGE CUPCAKES

MAKES 12 CUPCAKES

Nuts to You is a Canadian distributor of fine nut and seed butters. Their pumpkin seed nut butter is exquisite. Great texture and layered flavor. The figs add a level of sweetness that is unexpected but welcome.

⅓ cup (80 mL) pumpkin seed butter

½ cup (120 mL) coconut milk

¼ cup (60 mL) cocoa powder

1 cup (250 mL) brown sugar

¾ cup (180 mL) unbleached white flour

½ cup (120 mL) quinoa flour, toasted (see page 166, step 2)

½ cup (120 mL) thinly sliced dried figs

½ tsp (2 mL) baking powder

½ tsp (2 mL) sea salt

¼ tsp (1 mL) baking soda

2 large eggs, separated

1 tsp (5 mL) vanilla extract

1 cup (250 mL) yogurt

12 walnut halves

1. Preheat oven to 375°F (190°C). Line a 12-cup muffin pan with paper liners.

2. In a small saucepan, combine the pumpkin seed butter with the coconut milk. Bring to a boil over medium-high heat. Whisk until blended. Remove from heat. Add the cocoa powder. Whisk until smooth. Transfer to a large bowl. Let cool 5 minutes.

3. In a medium-size bowl, mix together the sugar, unbleached white flour and quinoa flour, figs, baking powder, salt, and baking soda.

4. Whisk the egg yolks, vanilla, and yogurt into the pumpkin seed mixture. Add the flour mixture and stir until just blended.

5. Beat the egg whites until stiff, using electric beaters. Fold into the batter.

6. Spoon into the prepared muffin cups, filling each cup three-quarters full. Top with walnut halves. Bake for 25 minutes.

NABALI OLIVE OIL

ORGANIC AND FAIR

CANAAN

PALESTINE

16.9 fl oz (1 pt 0.9 oz) / ℮ 500 ml

Chapter Seven

FAIR TRADE
OLIVE OIL

FAIR TRADE
OLIVE OIL

Palestinian Fair Trade Association

Name of producer co-op:
Our producer union is called the Palestine Fair Trade Association. It is the largest fair trade producers union in Palestine, with over 1,400 small-scale Palestinian farmers joined in fair trade collectives and cooperatives across the country. You can find all the cooperatives and the number of farmers in each cooperative in the union at the website www.palestinefairtrade.org.

Location:
Palestine Fair Trade Association—the union of farmers/producers association is located in Jenin, Palestine.
Canaan Fair Trade Company—the production, storage and sales/marketing, and exporter building is located in Burqin, Jenin, Palestine.

How did the co-op get started?
The Canaan Project started with the nonprofit organization PFTA, a union of fair trade producing cooperatives, producers, and exporters offering original landrace varieties of food products produced on small-scale family farms in Palestine. The association was founded in 2004 in Jenin and maintains offices there. We were the first Fairtrade-certified olive oil in the world.

How many members are in the co-op?
Canaan Palestine works with 52 olive oil producing cooperatives and over 1,400 farming families across the West Bank.

How many years have you been involved in olive harvesting?
15 years.

How many olive trees are harvested in a season?
Approximately 594,500 olive trees are harvested in a season from the farmers who are registered with us in the Palestine Fair Trade Association union only.

ABOVE Aida and Mahmoud Karam   **BELOW** Karam's family

How is the crop harvested? Manually or with machines?

The olive harvest season is the best season in Palestine. The olive harvest is a cultural heritage, and it's a family season where everyone goes to the fields from dawn to dark, harvesting the olive trees in their fields by hand. It's all done by hand—no machines are used to harvest, only a ladder, a shader (net) under the tree to collect all the olives as they fall, and a harvest comb that helps in harvesting.

Where is it sold?

The Canaan brand is available in the US through different distributors and wholesalers. We have a warehouse in New Jersey. Our products are available in different parts of Europe through different partners of Fairtrade that take co-branding products. Our partners are in the UK, Germany, Switzerland, Austria, and Sweden, and Canaan products are found at fine food specialty stores and in high-end retail outlets and chains around the world. We are also in Korea and Japan and the Gulf area in Kuwait. Not only do we offer packaged finished products, but we also work with distinctive brands on a global scale that rely on Canaan to source high-quality ingredients and support our ethos of nurturing life through our social responsibility and commitment to sustainable ecosystems.

Olive Oil History

From 6000 BCE, ancient peoples spread the olive tree along the shores of the Mediterranean. Historians over the ages have sung the praises of olive oil. Consider its many uses—as a fuel, for skincare, medicinal, and as a condiment. The olive tree is an evergreen, its leaves a light silvery green. The fruit has a fleshy pulp and its color ranges from black to mustard yellow and green. Due to its deep roots, it can withstand extreme temperatures, frost, and drought. It is well known for its longevity.

Today, Spain is the largest producer of olive oil in the world, and the region of Andalusia accounts for 75% of Spanish production. It is well known that Mediterranean people do not suffer from the same degree of obesity, cancer, bone, and heart problems as North Americans. Olive oil has been linked to a reduction in rates of cancers, positive effects on bone calcification, and a lowering of bad cholesterol in the blood, while leaving the good cholesterol intact.

Olive oil has potential in the prevention and control of diabetes and in warding off the effects of aging ("Olive Oil, Quality of Life," International Olive Oil Council). Health-inducing lycopene in tomatoes is more readily absorbed when paired with olive oil. Lycopene—a powerful antioxidant—is linked to the prevention of prostate, cervical, and digestive system cancers. Garlic, long revered as another potent antioxidant and a mainstay of alternative medicine, is the perfect flavor complement for both olive oil and tomatoes. It's a win-win pairing. Not only does olive oil taste terrific, it brings out the best in other ingredients, too. The health benefits of olive oil are backed by scientific research.

The biological and therapeutic value of olive oil is closely related to its chemical structure because its fatty acid content is well-balanced. On the one hand, it is rich in monounsaturated fats (between 60% and 80%), mainly oleic acid. An advantage to cooking with olive oil is that oleic acid is stable at higher temperatures, and this is important for preventing oxidation. It also contains polyunsaturated fats (omega-3 and -6 fatty acids), which are essential elements for the human diet that our body cannot synthesize. Lastly, its minor components (such as natural antioxidants and vitamins K and especially E) are also clearly beneficial and contribute to your health.

Because of its oleic acid content, olive oil is well-tolerated by the stomach and facilitates digestion. Two small tablespoons of olive oil on an empty stomach can help to relieve chronic constipation.

Olive oil is highly recommended for both the elderly and children. First, its essential fatty acid content is similar to that of mother's milk, and it assists in bone mineralization, development, and calcification. As part of a diet for the elderly, its high content of natural antioxidants creates a defense mechanism against oxidation processes, improving cardiovascular circulation and helping to slow down the aging of cells.

Olive oil is pressed from olives, which are, botanically speaking, a fresh fruit. The fact that it is a natural fruit juice is supported by the fact that, over the centuries, the fruit has continued to be picked and processed in the traditional manner.

We are learning what citizens of the Mediterranean have known for centuries. Olive oil is nature's own balm!

The Olive Oil Categories

Extra virgin olive oil is obtained solely by mechanical processing under special temperatures. It has not undergone any treatment other than washing, decantation, and filtration. It is the oily juice of the olive. Depending on its characteristics and acidity, it may be classified as extra virgin or virgin olive oil. With an excellent flavor and aroma, and a maximum acidity of 1%,

expressed in terms of oleic acid, it has an intense taste and is very appropriate for salads, raw vegetables, and cold dishes.

Refined olive oil is obtained by refining virgin olive oil until high acidity or inferior features are eliminated. It is used for blending with olive oil and presents high standings of aroma and flavor, with acidity below 2% of oleic acid.

Olive oil is a blend of refined olive oil and virgin olive oil that is fit for consumption without any further processing.

BROWN RICE BEET BURGERS

MAKES 6 TO 8 BURGERS

This is the perfect make-ahead mixture. You can serve this recipe as a burger, crumbled on pasta, as a little meatball, or inside a bun. Plain yogurt is my favorite condiment to serve with them. Tart and acidic, the yogurt balances the heat in the paprika. Serve baked or fried.

....

1. Preheat oven to 350°F (180°C). Line a rimmed baking sheet with parchment paper. Set aside.

2. In a medium-size pot, bring 2 cups (480 mL) stock to a boil. Add the rice. Return to a boil and lower heat to simmer. Cover and cook for 40 minutes, or until rice is soft.

3. In a small pot, bring the remaining 1 cup (250 mL) stock to a boil. Add the lentils. Return to a boil and lower heat to simmer. Cook for 15 to 20 minutes, or until lentils are tender.

4. In a medium-size skillet, heat 2 tbsp (30 mL) olive oil over medium-high heat. Add the onion and sauté for 5 to 8 minutes, or until the onion softens. Lower the heat to medium and add the beets, garlic, walnuts, cherries, lemon juice, paprika, ½ tsp (2 mL) salt, and ¼ tsp (1 mL) pepper. Cook for 8 to 10 minutes, stirring often.

5. In a large bowl, combine the beet–onion mixture with the cooked lentils and ½ tsp (2 mL) salt and ¼ tsp (1 mL) pepper.

6. Add the rice, egg, and dill to the bowl of a food processor. Pulse to form a coarse purée, about 15 to 20 seconds.

7. Add the rice mixture to the beet–onion mixture and mix well.

8. Divide the burger mixture into 8 portions. Place the burgers on the prepared baking sheet. Bake for 12 to 15 minutes. Remove from the oven and serve, or continue with the recipe and brown the burgers in olive oil.

9. Heat a large skillet over medium-high heat with 3 tbsp (45 mL) olive oil. Place 4 or 5 burgers in the skillet and cook for 5 minutes. Flip the burgers over and reduce heat to low. Cover and cook the burgers for 5 more minutes. They will have a brown crust. Use 2 tbsp (30 mL) oil to cook the remaining burgers.

10. Serve with yogurt and your favorite condiments.

---

3 cups (700 mL) vegetable stock, divided

1 cup (250 mL) short grain brown rice, rinsed

½ cup (120 mL) black or brown lentils, rinsed

7 tbsp (105 mL) olive oil, divided

1 large Vidalia onion, diced

1 cup (250 mL) grated, peeled beets (1 large beet or 4 small)

4 garlic cloves, finely chopped

1 cup (250 mL) walnuts, chopped

½ cup (120 mL) dried cherries

1½ tbsp (22 mL) fresh lemon juice

1 tsp (5 mL) smoked paprika

1 tsp (5 mL) sea salt, divided

½ tsp (2 mL) ground black pepper, divided

1 large egg

¼ cup (60 mL) fresh dill, minced

1 cup (250 mL) plain yogurt

MUSHROOM TART WITH BROWN RICE CRUST

MAKES 6 SERVINGS

1½ tbsp (22 mL) olive oil

1 cup (250 mL) long grain brown rice

2 cups (480 mL) vegetable stock

2 large egg whites

3 tbsp (45 mL) salted butter, divided

1 large onion, diced

½ tsp (2 mL) dried oregano

4 cups (950 mL) assorted fresh mushrooms, sliced

1 tbsp (15 mL) all-purpose flour

½ cup (120 mL) milk

1 large egg

2 tomatoes, thinly sliced

½ cup (120 mL) grated cheddar cheese

¼ cup (60 mL) chives, thinly sliced

I like long grain brown rice the best. It cooks up light and fluffy with distinct grains and provides an excellent crust for this tart. Delicious hot or cold.

1. Preheat oven to 350°F (180°C). Coat a 9-inch (23 cm) pie dish with 1½ tbsp (22 mL) olive oil.

2. Rinse the brown rice in a fine mesh colander under cold water and drain. Bring the stock to a boil in a medium-size pot over high heat. Stir in the rinsed rice. Cover, reduce heat, and simmer for 45 minutes, or until the rice is tender.

3. In a medium-size bowl, whisk the egg whites until frothy. Add the rice. Press the mixture into the bottom and up the sides of the pie plate. Bake for 10 minutes.

4. In a large skillet, heat 2 tbsp (30 mL) butter over medium heat. Add the onion and oregano. Sauté for 5 minutes. Add the mushrooms, 1 cup (250 mL) at a time. Sauté for 3 to 5 minutes. Mushrooms will release their liquid and provide a base of moisture for the next addition. Sauté until all the liquid has evaporated, about 3 minutes. Transfer to a bowl.

5. Heat the remaining 1 tbsp (15 mL) butter in the same skillet over medium heat. Stir in the flour. Gradually add the milk and cook for 3 minutes, or until thickened, stirring constantly. Whisk in the egg. Remove from heat and fold into the mushroom mixture.

6. Pour the filling into the crust. Add a layer of sliced tomatoes, followed by the cheese, and sprinkle chives over top. Bake 30 minutes. Let sit 10 minutes before serving.

SPICED BASMATI RICE WITH ROASTED VEGETABLES

MAKES 4 TO 6 SERVINGS

This dish is served upside down. You flip the contents out of the pot and the rice forms a supporting layer. Use a dish towel to fit over the lid of the pot. It catches condensation as the rice steams and helps the rice to become fluffy and separated as opposed to mushy and wet. A great way to cook rice. You can serve this dish with chicken, fish, or just on its own.

....

1. Preheat oven to 350°F (180°C).

2. Line 2 rimmed baking sheets with parchment paper. Place the eggplant and peppers (skin side down) on 2 separate sheets. Add the unpeeled garlic cloves to the pepper sheet, distributing evenly. Drizzle each pan with 2 tbsp (30 mL) olive oil and ½ tsp (2 mL) salt. Bake both sheets for 20 minutes; add the tomatoes to the peppers. Bake for an additional 10 minutes.

3. Rinse the rice in cold water, using a fine mesh strainer. Place in a large bowl of cold water and soak for 10 minutes. Drain and set aside.

4. Remove the vegetables from the oven. Allow to cool and remove skins from the garlic cloves.

5. In a medium-size pot, bring the vegetable stock to a boil. Add the cumin, turmeric, coriander, cinnamon, allspice, and ½ tsp (2 mL) salt. Stir well. Lower the heat and simmer.

6. In a large saucepan over medium heat, melt the butter. Add the baked eggplant. Add the tomatoes, roasted garlic, and peppers on top of the eggplant. Add the rice and hot stock. Bring to a boil, reduce heat to a simmer, and cover the pan with a clean dish towel and lid. Cook for 25 minutes. Switch off the heat and allow to rest for 5 minutes.

7. To serve, remove the lid and dish towel. Place a large serving platter on top of the saucepan and invert the pan. Remove the pan; sprinkle with cilantro and pine nuts.

2 medium eggplants, sliced into ½-inch (1 cm) slices

3 red or yellow peppers, cut in half lengthwise and remove stem, membrane, and seeds

2 garlic bulbs, separated into cloves with skins on (about 20 cloves)

¼ cup (60 mL) olive oil, divided

1½ tsp (7 mL) sea salt, divided

3 large tomatoes, thickly sliced

2½ cups (600 mL) vegetable stock

1½ cups (350 mL) basmati rice

1 tsp (5 mL) ground cumin

1 tsp (5 mL) ground turmeric

1 tsp (5 mL) ground coriander

½ tsp (2 mL) ground cinnamon

½ tsp (2 mL) ground allspice

3 tbsp (45 mL) salted butter

¼ cup (60 mL) cilantro, finely chopped

¼ cup (60 mL) toasted pine nuts (see page 197)

BEAN SOUP WITH LEEKS AND FREEKEH

MAKES 4 TO 6 SERVINGS

¼ cup (60 mL) olive oil, divided

2 leeks, thinly sliced, white and pale green parts only

3 garlic cloves, finely chopped

1 tsp (5 mL) ground coriander

1 tsp (5 mL) ground cumin

½ tsp (2 mL) ground allspice

One 19-oz (540 mL) can black beans, drained and rinsed

1 cup (250 mL) freekeh

1 medium parsnip, peeled and sliced into rounds

1 medium carrot, peeled and sliced into rounds

2 celery stalks, cut into ½-inch (1 cm) pieces

8 cups (2 L) vegetable stock

½ tsp (2 mL) sea salt

⅛ tsp (0.5 mL) black pepper

2 tbsp (30 mL) freshly squeezed lemon juice

½ cup (120 mL) 2% plain yogurt

3 tbsp (45 mL) finely chopped chives

Freekeh is an ancient grain made from unripe green wheat. The outer husk is burnt off and a pliable, slightly chewy whole grain is left that is similar in texture to coarse bulgur. The freekeh and olive oil in this book are from Canaan Fair Trade, a Palestinian producer co-op (since 2004).

1. In a large saucepan, heat 2 tbsp (30 mL) oil over medium heat. Add the leeks and garlic, and sauté 3 to 5 minutes, or until softened. Add the coriander, cumin, and allspice. Fry for 2 minutes, stirring.

2. Add the beans, freekeh, parsnip, carrot, celery, and stock. Bring to a boil, lower heat, cover, and simmer for 40 minutes. Add the salt, pepper, lemon juice, and remaining 2 tbsp (30 mL) olive oil. Stir well and simmer for 2 more minutes.

3. Ladle into bowls. Add 2 tbsp (30 mL) yogurt to each bowl and a sprinkling of chives.

FAIR TRADE ZA'ATAR

MAKES ½ CUP (120 ML)

Za'atar is a Middle Eastern spice mixture made from thyme, sesame, and sumac. Sumac is the powder from the tart berry of the sumac tree. It is reddish-purple and dried and ground into a powder. I am using it here to make crunchy aromatic croutons to top the Bean Soup with Leeks and Freekeh (see page 184). I would also recommend the Canaan za'atar spice mixture. Made with wild thyme from the West Bank, it is flavorful and one of the best prepackaged spice mixtures I have ever used.

....

1. In a spice grinder or with a mortar and pestle, combine the thyme, oregano, sesame seeds, sumac, and salt. Pulse and grind until you break up the seeds and have a coarse powder. Store in the fridge and use within a week. To serve, top with croutons and fresh parsley.

2 tbsp (30 mL) dried thyme

2 tbsp (30 mL) dried oregano

3 tbsp (45 mL) toasted pine nuts (see page 197)

1 tbsp (15 mL) ground sumac

¼ tsp (1 mL) kosher salt

4 Za'atar Croutons (see below) per bowl

2 tbsp (30 mL) fresh parsley, chopped per bowl

ZA'ATAR CROUTONS

MAKES 2 CUPS (480 ML)

1. Slice the bread into 1-inch (2.5 cm) pieces.

2. In a large frying pan, heat the oil over high heat. Once it is hot, add the bread and toast for 1 minute on all sides. Sprinkle za'atar over the bread and fry for 3 to 5 minutes, until it's toasted and crunchy. Dry the croutons on paper towels to soak up any excess oil.

3 cups (700 mL) cubed bread

⅓ cup (80 mL) olive oil

2 tbsp (30 mL) za'atar

PARSNIP HUMMUS

MAKES 2 CUPS (480 ML)

1 lb (454 g) medium-size parsnips, sliced into 1-inch (2.5 cm) pieces

¾ cup (180 mL) vegetable stock or water

¼ cup (60 mL) tahini

¼ cup (60 mL) extra virgin olive oil

2 tbsp (30 mL) lemon juice

2 garlic cloves, minced

1 tsp (5 mL) smoked paprika

½ tsp (2 mL) ground coriander

½ tsp (2 mL) ground cumin

½ tsp (2 mL) sea salt

⅛ tsp (0.5 mL) ground black pepper

2 tbsp (30 mL) toasted sesame seeds

Hummus is not just about chickpeas! You can use tahini, olive oil, garlic, and lemon juice and still create a creamy, delicious dip that is full of flavor. Look for firm, medium-size parsnips with smooth surfaces.

1. Add enough water to reach the bottom of a collapsible steamer set in a saucepan and bring to a boil on high heat. Place the parsnips in the steamer basket, cover, and steam for 8 to 10 minutes. Remove from the basket and transfer to a food processor.

2. Purée the parsnips in a food processor, then add the stock, tahini, olive oil, lemon juice, garlic, paprika, coriander, cumin, salt, and pepper and process until completely smooth, at least 1 minute.

3. Transfer to a small bowl. Allow to sit at room temperature for 20 minutes. Drizzle with extra olive oil and sesame seeds. If the mixture becomes too thick (after being in the fridge), stir in 1 tbsp (15 mL) room temperature stock or water to loosen before serving.

4. Serve with sliced vegetables, corn chips, or crackers.

BRAISED EGGPLANT IN TOMATO SAUCE

MAKES 4 TO 6 SERVINGS

3 tbsp (45 mL) extra
virgin olive oil

1 large Vidalia onion, diced

1 cup (250 mL) button
mushrooms, thinly sliced

4 medium Japanese eggplants,
halved lengthwise and cut into
1-inch (2.5 cm) pieces

3 medium-size garlic
cloves, minced

1 cup (250 mL) vegetable stock
or water

1 tsp (5 mL) ground cumin

½ tsp (2 mL) ground allspice

½ tsp (2 mL) sea salt

2½ cups (600 mL) tomato sauce
or whole peeled tomatoes

2 tbsp (30 mL) red wine vinegar

One 14-oz (398 mL) can
cannellini beans, drained

3 tbsp (45 mL) basil,
chopped

The secret is to slow cook the eggplant in tomato sauce until it has a silky texture and is incredibly tender. You need a pot that can go from stovetop to oven, often known as a Dutch oven.

....

1. Preheat oven to 325°F (160°C).

2. Heat oil in a Dutch oven over medium-high heat. Add the onion and sauté 5 to 7 minutes, or until soft. Add the mushrooms, eggplant, garlic, and vegetable stock and cook for 5 minutes.

3. Add the cumin, allspice, salt, and tomato sauce. Cook for 2 minutes more.

4. Stir in the vinegar; reduce heat to medium-low and cook for 5 minutes.

5. Add the beans. Cover and transfer the pot to the preheated oven. Cook for 40 to 45 minutes, or until eggplant is tender. Stir in the chopped basil.

MUHAMMARA

MAKES 2⅓ CUPS (545 ML)

This is my absolute favorite roasted red pepper dip. Use this recipe as a sauce for lasagna or as a dip. Sweet, smoky, and savory, your choice of fair trade olive oil will elevate this recipe. Serve with corn chips, pita, and sliced vegetables

···

1. Using a food processor, pulse the almonds. Remove from the food processor and place in a small bowl. Pulse the red peppers, breadcrumbs, lemon juice, oil, molasses, sugar, salt, cumin, and cayenne until smooth, 1 to 2 minutes. Add the ground almonds. Pulse for 30 seconds or until combined. Sprinkle with basil.

1 cup (250 mL) almonds or walnuts, toasted

2 cups (480 mL) jarred roasted red peppers, rinsed and drained

¼ cup (60 mL) dry breadcrumbs

3 tbsp (45 mL) freshly squeezed lemon juice

2 tbsp (30 mL) extra virgin olive oil

1 tbsp (15 mL) molasses

1 tsp (5 mL) brown sugar

½ tsp (2 mL) sea salt

½ tsp (2 mL) ground cumin

⅛ tsp (0.5 mL) cayenne pepper

1 tbsp (15 mL) minced fresh basil, sprinkle on top

RED LENTIL SOUP WITH FAIR TRADE SPICES

MAKES 10 CUPS (2.5 L)

Red lentils dissolve into a creamy, thick purée when cooked that is very satisfying. Using Cha's Organic spices from Sri Lanka (cumin, ginger, cinnamon), this recipe is a mesh of Far East flavors.

3 tbsp (45 mL) extra virgin olive oil

1 large Vidalia onion, finely chopped

1 tsp (5 mL) smoked paprika

½ tsp (2 mL) sea salt

½ tsp (2 mL) ground coriander

½ tsp (2 mL) ground cumin

¼ tsp (1 mL) ground ginger

¼ tsp (1 mL) ground cinnamon

⅛ tsp (0.5 mL) black pepper

1 tbsp (15 mL) tomato paste

2 medium-size garlic cloves, finely diced

6 cups (1.5 L) vegetable broth

2 cups (480 mL) red lentils, rinsed

2 tbsp (30 mL) freshly squeezed lemon juice

½ cup (120 mL) fresh chopped cilantro

1. Heat oil in a large saucepan over medium heat. Add the onion, paprika, and salt. Cook, stirring occasionally, for 5 minutes or until soft. Stir in the coriander, cumin, ginger, cinnamon, and pepper. Cook for 2 more minutes, stirring. Add the tomato paste and garlic and cook for 1 minute.

2. Stir in the broth and lentils and bring to a boil. Reduce heat to a simmer, cover, and cook, stirring often, for 15 minutes or until soft.

3. Whisk the soup until the texture resembles a coarse purée, about a minute. Stir in the lemon juice and garnish with cilantro leaves.

A NOTE ABOUT RED LENTILS

Red lentils (they are orange in color) cook in 20 to 25 minutes and lose their disc shape. Creamy, they have a porridge-like consistency. They cannot be used in place of green, black, or brown lentils, which hold their shape and have a different texture that is not at all creamy.

LENTIL PISTACHIO BURGERS

MAKES 6 SERVINGS

1 cup (250 mL) green or black
lentils, rinsed

2 cups (480 mL) vegetable stock

¾ cup (180 mL)
pistachios, shelled

½ cup (120 mL) plain dry
breadcrumbs

3 medium-size garlic
cloves, minced

1 tsp (5 mL) ground cumin

1 tsp (5 mL) ground coriander

1 tsp (5 mL) sea salt

½ tsp (2 mL) red pepper flakes

¼ tsp (1 mL) black pepper

6 tbsp (90 mL) olive oil, divided

2 large eggs

Once you bake these burgers, you can serve them or sauté them in
olive oil to crisp and brown their skin. Sliced tomatoes, pickles, and a
tangy yogurt sauce complement these burgers so well.

....

1. Preheat oven to 350°F (180°C). Line a rimmed baking sheet with
parchment paper.

2. Combine the lentils and stock in a saucepan. Bring to a boil over
high heat. Reduce heat to medium and simmer for 20 minutes, or until
tender. Drain in a colander and set aside.

3. In a food processor, combine the pistachios, breadcrumbs, garlic,
cumin, coriander, salt, red pepper flakes, and pepper. Process until
finely ground. Add the cooked lentils and 1 tbsp (15 mL) olive oil. Pulse
until coarsely chopped.

4. Whisk the egg in a large bowl. Add the lentil mixture. Mix well.
Divide into 6 equal parts. Roll into balls and flatten with the palm of
your hand into ¾-inch (2 cm) patties.

5. Bake for 10 minutes. Heat 3 tbsp (45 mL) olive oil in a large skillet.
Add 4 burgers. Cook over medium-low heat until crisp and browned,
turning gently, 6 to 8 minutes per side. Repeat with the remaining
burgers, using the remaining 2 tbsp (30 mL) oil and adding more oil
if necessary.

TANGY YOGURT SAUCE

MAKES 1 CUP (250 ML)

¾ cup (180 mL) full-fat yogurt

2 tbsp (30 mL) cilantro
leaves, chopped

1 tbsp (15 mL) fresh lemon juice

¼ tsp (1 mL) sea salt

⅛ tsp (0.5 mL) black pepper

1. In a medium-size bowl, whisk together the yogurt, cilantro, and
lemon juice. Add salt and pepper. Stir well

ROASTED CAULIFLOWER WITH CUMIN AND TURMERIC

MAKES 4 SERVINGS

Turmeric has such a vibrant color. The deep yellow goes so well with the green herbs. Delicious hot or cold, easy to reheat, this is a great side dish or pita stuffer.

....

1. Preheat oven to 425°F (220°C). In a medium-size bowl, combine ¼ cup (60 mL) olive oil with the cumin, turmeric, red pepper flakes, and salt. Toss the cauliflower with the oil mixture.

2. Place the cauliflower florets on a rimmed baking sheet lined with parchment paper. Spread the cauliflower in an even layer. Drizzle the remaining 1 tbsp (15 mL) olive oil over top and bake for 30 minutes until browned and tender.

3. Toast the pine nuts in a small heavy-bottomed skillet over medium heat. Stir and toss the nuts for 2 to 3 minutes or until lightly browned.

4. Transfer the cauliflower to a medium-size bowl. Garnish with toasted pine nuts, cilantro, and mint.

TOASTING NUTS AND SEEDS (STOVETOP AND OVEN)

Toasting nuts and seeds is a technique that intensifies their flavor and deepens their color. Toasting may be done in the oven or on the stovetop. I do not use any oil or butter in the toasting process. I prefer to toast my nuts and seeds in a large heavy-bottomed skillet over medium-high heat. It is important to stir your nuts or seeds several times with a wooden spoon to expose all sides. They release an aroma and turn darker as they toast, and seeds will also pop and crackle. Nuts take 5 to 6 minutes, seeds and pine nuts about 2 to 4 minutes. Watch them closely and stir often.

If you prefer to use the oven, preheat to 350°F (180°C). Line a rimmed baking sheet with parchment paper. Spread the nuts or seeds out on the sheet and toast them in the middle of the oven until golden brown, 6 to 8 minutes for nuts and 4 to 6 minutes for seeds. Check every few minutes to ensure they do not burn

5 tbsp (75 mL) olive oil, divided

1½ tsp (7 mL) ground cumin

1 tsp (5 mL) ground turmeric

¾ tsp (4 mL) red pepper flakes

¾ tsp (4 mL) sea salt

1 medium cauliflower, halved, cored, and cut into 1-inch (2.5 cm) florets (about 8 cups/2 L)

¼ cup (60 mL) toasted pine nuts (see below)

2 tbsp (30 mL) cilantro, chopped

2 tsp (10 mL) fresh mint, chopped

SALMON AND POTATO CAKES WITH DILL

MAKES 8 CAKES

1 lb (454 g) medium-size Yukon Gold potatoes, scrubbed

⅓ cup (80 mL) olive oil, divided

½ lb (227 g) skinless salmon

½ tsp (2 mL) sea salt

⅛ tsp (0.5 mL) black pepper

3 green onions, chopped

2 large eggs, lightly beaten

2 garlic cloves, minced

1 tbsp (15 mL) fresh ginger root, minced

1 tbsp (15 mL) fresh dill, minced

Half a medium red onion, finely chopped

2 tsp (10 mL) tamari

2 tsp (10 mL) toasted sesame oil

½ cup (120 mL) plain dry breadcrumbs

Here is a recipe for breakfast or dinner. Salmon potato cakes can be eaten warm or cold. Easy to prepare—I almost feel Scandinavian.

....

1. Preheat oven to 350°F (180°C). Line a rimmed baking sheet with parchment paper.

2. Bring a large pot of salted water to a boil over high heat. Add the potatoes. Cover and reduce heat to medium-low. Simmer for 20 minutes or until potatoes are tender when pierced with the tip of a knife. Drain. Let cool, then peel. Transfer the potatoes to a large bowl and mash.

3. Oil parchment paper with 1 tsp (5 mL) olive oil. Place the salmon on the baking sheet. Season with salt and pepper. Bake for 15 minutes until salmon is medium-rare.

4. Flake the salmon and add to the potato mixture. Add the green onions, eggs, garlic, ginger, dill, onion, tamari, and sesame oil. Mix well. Fold in the breadcrumbs. Form into eight ½-cup (120 mL) patties.

5. In a large nonstick pan, heat half of the remaining oil over medium-high heat. Fry the potato cakes until browned and crisp, about 2 minutes per side. Transfer to a rimmed baking sheet lined with parchment paper. Repeat with the remaining potato cakes, adding more oil if necessary.

6. Bake the salmon cakes for 10 to 15 minutes at 350°F (180°C) until heated through.

CHICKPEA COUSCOUS TABBOULEH

MAKES 6 SERVINGS

This recipe is so fast to prepare. You can add olives, feta, and chives.

....

1. Bring the water or stock to a boil. Add the couscous. Stir and cover. Remove from stove and let stand for 5 minutes. Place in a large bowl.

2. In a small bowl, whisk the shallot, lemon juice, mustard, garlic, salt, and pepper. Gradually whisk in the olive oil until combined. Stir into the couscous.

3. Stir in the tomatoes, chickpeas, cucumber, parsley, and mint. Toss to combine.

4. Garnish with pine nuts.

2 cups (480 mL) water or vegetable stock

1 cup (250 mL) whole wheat couscous

1 shallot, finely chopped

2 tbsp (30 mL) fresh lemon juice

1 tbsp (15 mL) Dijon mustard

2 small garlic cloves, finely chopped

¼ tsp (1 mL) sea salt

⅛ tsp (0.5 mL) ground black pepper

½ cup (120 mL) olive oil

1 cup (250 mL) cherry tomatoes, halved

1 cup (250 mL) cooked chickpeas

Half an English cucumber, diced

2 tbsp (30 mL) flat-leaf parsley, chopped

2 tbsp (30 mL) fresh mint, chopped

½ cup (120 mL) toasted pine nuts (see page 197)

DRIED FRUIT AND SPICE MUFFINS

MAKES 12 MUFFINS

½ cup (120 mL) 2% milk

½ cup (120 mL) maple syrup

½ cup (120 mL) diced fresh
pineapple with juice

¼ cup (60 mL) olive oil

2 cups (480 mL) unbleached
white flour

1 tsp (5 mL) baking powder

½ tsp (2 mL) sea salt

1 tsp (5 mL) ground cinnamon

¼ tsp (1 mL) ground nutmeg

¼ tsp (1 mL) ground cloves

¾ cup (180 mL) dried cherries

½ cup (120 mL) raisins
or currants

¾ cup (180 mL) walnuts,
toasted

Aromatic spices and dried fruit impart such a luscious taste to every bite. They bring out the best in each other—not too sweet and oh so fragrant!

1. Preheat oven to 375°F (190°C). Lightly grease a 12-cup muffin tin or line it with paper liners.

2. In a medium-size bowl, mix the milk, maple syrup, pineapple, and oil.

3. In a large bowl, mix the flour, baking powder, salt, cinnamon, nutmeg, and cloves. Add the pineapple mixture. Stir until just combined.

4. Sprinkle with cherries, raisins, and walnuts. Fold until combined.

5. Spoon the mixture into the prepared muffin tin. Bake for 20 to 25 minutes.

TIP: Dried fruit should be treated as a perishable ingredient with a long shelf life. Store dried fruit in airtight containers at room temperature away from light, heat, and above all moisture. Stored properly, it should last at least 4 months. If fresh pineapple is not available, you can use any fresh or frozen berry.

BABY POTATO SALAD

MAKES 6 TO 8 SERVINGS

There are so many types of mini potato to buy. My favorite is a multicolored package with purple and red mini potatoes. Delicious hot or cold.

....

1. Halve the potatoes. Place in a large saucepan; fill with water. Bring to a boil and reduce heat to medium-high. Cook for 5 minutes or until tender.

2. Add the asparagus and frozen peas; return to a simmer. Cook, stirring occasionally, until asparagus is tender-crisp and potatoes are tender, another 3 minutes. Drain and set aside in a medium-size bowl.

3. Whisk the egg yolk and vinegar in a large bowl; season with salt. Whisking constantly, gradually add the oil, drop by drop at first, then whisk until the mayonnaise is thick and creamy. Whisk in the mustard.

4. Add the potato–asparagus mixture to the bowl and toss to coat. Add shallot and chives. Toss gently to combine.

2 lbs (1 kg) mini potatoes

14 spears asparagus, trimmed and cut into 2-inch (5 cm) lengths

1 cup (250 mL) frozen peas

1 large egg yolk

2 tsp (10 mL) white wine vinegar

¼ tsp (1 mL) sea salt

⅓ cup (80 mL) olive oil

2 tbsp (30 mL) Dijon mustard

1 small shallot, diced

2 tbsp (30 mL) chopped fresh chives

WATERMELON, OLIVE, AND MANCHEGO CHEESE SALAD

MAKES 6 TO 8 SERVINGS

⅓ cup (80 mL) olive oil

2 tbsp (30 mL) fresh lemon juice

1 large shallot, finely diced

6 cups (1.5 L) cubed (1-inch/2.5-cm pieces) seedless watermelon, removed from rind

1 medium English cucumber, cubed, with peel (½-inch/1-cm pieces)

⅓ cup (80 mL) chopped pitted black olives

3 tbsp (45 mL) finely chopped fresh mint

¾ cup (180 mL) grated Manchego cheese

The sweet salty flavor is the perfect taste on a hot summer day. Feel free to add more mint or other leftover melon to this recipe. Watermelon retains its crisp texture once it has been marinated, but only for the next few hours.

....

1. In a small bowl, add the oil, lemon juice, and shallot. Whisk to blend.

2. In a large bowl, combine the watermelon, cucumber, and olives. Pour the dressing over the watermelon–cucumber mixture and toss to coat.

3. Add the mint and Manchego cheese.

PEANUT SLAW
WITH EDAMAME, ORANGE, AND BASIL

MAKES ½ CUP (120 ML)

The crunch in this salad is incredible. I like to add the dressing to the amount I am serving. The leftover salad retains its crunch without the dressing and you avoid soggy leftovers. The colors are so brilliant.

....

1. Place the cabbage, mango, apple, celery, and basil in a large bowl. Toss well.

2. In a small pot, bring 2 cups (480 mL) water to a boil. Add the edamame and cook for 5 minutes. Drain and cool. Add to the cabbage slaw.

3. In a medium-size bowl, whisk together the vinegar, mustard, honey, salt, and pepper. Slowly whisk in the oil until well-combined.

4. Add the dressing to the slaw salad and toss well. Add peanuts to garnish.

1 lb (454 g) red cabbage, halved, cored, and very thinly sliced

1½ cups (350 mL) diced mango, fresh or frozen, sliced into ½-inch (1 cm) pieces

1 large honey crisp apple, thinly sliced

2 celery stalks, thinly sliced

¼ cup (60 mL) chopped fresh basil

1 cup (250 mL) frozen shelled edamame

1 cup (250 mL) roasted salted peanuts for garnish

DRESSING

¼ cup (60 mL) apple cider vinegar

2 tsp (10 mL) Dijon mustard

1 tsp (5 mL) honey

¼ tsp (1 mL) sea salt

⅛ tsp (0.5 mL) black pepper

¼ cup (60 mL) olive oil

KALE CAESAR WITH CRISPY SPICED CHICKPEAS

MAKES 6 SERVINGS

1 lb (454 g) kale, sliced into very thin ribbon strips

One 19-oz (540 mL) can chickpeas (no salt added), drained

⅓ cup (80 mL) olive oil

1 tsp (5 mL) smoked paprika

1 tsp (5 mL) ground cumin

1 tsp (5 mL) sea salt

½ cup (120 mL) raw almonds, halved

½ cup (120 mL) raw sunflower seeds

½ cup (120 mL) raw pumpkin seeds

DRESSING

1 tbsp (15 mL) fresh lemon juice

2 tbsp (30 mL) Worcestershire sauce (see vegetarian version, page 208)

1 tsp (5 mL) Dijon mustard

½ tsp (2 mL) minced garlic (1 clove)

3 tbsp (45 mL) grated Parmesan cheese or good-tasting nutritional yeast

¼ cup (60 mL) olive oil

Will spicy chickpeas ever take the place of bacon? In this salad, the contrasting flavors (sweet and smoky) and textures (creamy and crunchy) make a very satisfying salad. Don't dress the salad until you are ready to serve. The kale quickly absorbs the dressing and you want it to be crisp. Worcestershire sauce contains anchovies. I have a vegan version of the recipe on the next page.

1. Preheat oven to 400°F (200°C).

2. If your kale has large leaves, place your knife against the stem and slice off the leaf on either side. Discard stems. Thinly slice the leaves. If kale leaves are small and the stem has not developed, trim the very end of the stem and thinly slice the rest. Rinse kale and store in a salad spinner.

3. In a medium-size bowl, combine the chickpeas, oil, paprika, cumin, and sea salt. Spread out in a single layer on a rimmed baking sheet lined with parchment paper. Roast for 30 minutes, stirring once.

4. Add the almonds, stir, and roast for another 8 to 10 minutes. Add the sunflower and pumpkin seeds. Roast for 5 more minutes, until brown and crisp.

5. Remove from the oven and pour into a small bowl.

6. In a medium-size bowl, combine the lemon juice, Worcestershire sauce, mustard, garlic, and Parmesan. Whisk until combined. Continue whisking as you add the olive oil. Dressing can be made ahead of time and stored in a covered jar in the refrigerator for 1 week. Makes ¾ cup (180 mL).

7. Place the kale leaves in a large bowl or platter. Add the roasted chickpea and nut mixture.

8. Dress the salad 5 minutes before serving.

VEGAN WORCESTERSHIRE SAUCE

MAKES 1 CUP (250 ML)

¼ cup (60 mL) water

¼ cup (60 mL) molasses

¼ cup (60 mL) tamari

3 tbsp (45 mL) apple cider vinegar

1 medium shallot, minced

1 tsp (5 mL) finely diced garlic

½ tsp (2 mL) peeled fresh
ginger root, finely diced

½ tsp (2 mL) ground ginger

½ tsp (2 mL) sea salt

⅛ tsp (0.5 mL) cayenne pepper

⅛ tsp (0.5 mL) ground cloves

This sauce does not contain anchovies (fish), and combining molasses with apple cider vinegar gives the sauce a sweet acidic balance reminiscent of the flavor of Worcestershire sauce.

....

1. In a medium-size saucepan, combine the water, molasses, tamari, vinegar, shallot, garlic, fresh ginger, ground ginger, salt, cayenne, and cloves.

2. Bring to a boil over medium-high heat, stirring often for 2 minutes.

3. Pour the mixture into a blender and blend for 1 minute until smooth. Mixture can be stored for 2 months in an airtight container in the fridge.

OLIVE, FIG, AND PECAN DIP

MAKES 1½ CUPS (350 ML)

A sweet and salty dip that can be served in celery crevices or on top of flatbreads. Can also be used as a condiment for burgers and falafel.

....

1. Place the olives, pecans, figs, capers, oil, honey, and vinegar in a food processor and purée for 30 seconds.

2. Let stand for 20 minutes for the flavors to combine.

1 cup (250 mL) pitted black olives

¾ cup (180 mL) pecans

5 small dried figs, stalks removed

2 tsp (10 mL) capers, rinsed and drained

¼ cup (60 mL) olive oil

1½ tsp (7 mL) honey

1 tsp (5 mL) apple cider vinegar

BLACK BEAN DIP

MAKES 2 CUPS (480 ML)

This is my favorite kitchen staple to have around. Spread it on a tortilla with a little cheese and salsa, eat it for breakfast over toast, or scoop it up with a tortilla chip. Easy to prepare, with a lot of flavor.

....

1. Heat the oil in a large saucepan over medium heat. Add the onion and cook, stirring often, until softened, 3 to 5 minutes.

2. Add the garlic, chili powder, salt, and cumin. Cook, stirring constantly, for 2 minutes.

3. Add the beans and bean liquid and cook until heated through, 3 to 5 minutes.

4. Remove from heat and purée in a food processor.

2 tbsp (30 mL) olive oil

1 large Vidalia onion, finely chopped

3 large garlic cloves, minced

4 tsp (20 mL) chili powder

1 tsp (5 mL) sea salt

1 tsp (5 mL) ground cumin

One 19-oz (540 mL) can black beans, drain and reserve ¼ cup (60 mL) bean liquid

GARLIC BRAISED SWISS CHARD

MAKES 4 SERVINGS

2 bunches (20 cups/5 L) red chard, stems and ribs removed

3 tbsp (45 mL) olive oil
+ 1 tbsp (15 mL) for a drizzle

4 medium garlic cloves, minced

½ tsp (2 mL) red chili flakes

1 cup (250 mL) canned chickpeas, rinsed

½ cup (120 mL) roasted red peppers, rinsed and thinly sliced

3 tbsp (45 mL) fresh lemon juice

½ tsp (2 mL) sea salt

⅛ tsp (0.5 mL) black pepper

This recipe goes well as a base for pasta sauce or a side dish for meat or fish. I like to remove the stems from the chard by trimming the stem ends first. Holding the leaf in one hand, tear the leaves from the stem in bite-size pieces. You can use a knife or scissors as well. Stems take longer to cook and can be too chewy. Save the stems for soup stock.

· ·

1. Wash the chard and leave wet. Remove the leaves from the ribs and tear the leaves into bite-size pieces.

2. Keep the leaves, stem, and ribs separate. Use the stems and ribs for future soup stock.

3. In a large skillet or wok, heat the olive oil over medium heat. Add the garlic and red chili flakes and swirl in the oil for 30 seconds.

4. Add 2 cups (480 mL) chard and stir, adding more as the chard wilts. When all the leaves have wilted, add the chickpeas, peppers, lemon juice, salt, and pepper. Cover, reduce heat to low, and cook for 5 minutes.

5. Transfer to a serving bowl with a slotted spoon and drizzle with 1 tbsp (15 mL) olive oil.

TEMPEH MANGO STIR FRY

MAKES 4 TO 6 SERVINGS

Tempeh is a high-protein cultured food made from soybeans and grains, and is available fresh or frozen. It is made by culturing cooked, cracked soybeans with the culture Rhizopus oligosporus. The fermentation process enhances the flavor and makes the soybeans easier to digest. Spicy and sweet, serve it with rice or quinoa.

....

1. In a medium-size saucepan, heat 3 tbsp (45 mL) olive oil over high heat. Stir-fry the tempeh for 6 to 8 minutes, or until golden on all sides. Transfer tempeh to a small bowl.

2. In another small bowl, combine the orange juice, 6 tbsp (90 mL) water, jalapeno, tamari, and ginger. Set aside.

3. In a wok, heat the remaining 1 tbsp (15 mL) oil over high heat. Add the onion and cook, stirring briskly, for 2 minutes. Stir in the parsnip and cook, stirring briskly, for 2 minutes. Stir in the carrot, broccoli, and remaining water and cook, stirring, for 2 minutes. Add the peas and cook for 2 more minutes, or until vegetables are tender crisp. Slide vegetables to the side of the wok.

4. Whisk the cornstarch into the orange juice mixture and pour into the center of the wok. Reduce heat to medium and cook, stirring constantly, for about 2 minutes, or until the sauce is thickened. Add the mango and cooked tempeh and heat through, stirring to combine ingredients.

5. Meanwhile, break noodles in half into a medium-size bowl. In a small pot, bring 2 cups (480 mL) water to a boil. Pour the boiling water over the noodles. Let stand 4 minutes; drain.

6. Divide the noodles into 6 portions and spoon the stir-fry over top. Garnish with mint.

¼ cup (60 mL) olive oil, divided

One 8-oz (227 g) package tempeh, cut into ½-inch (1 cm) cubes

¾ cup (180 mL) freshly squeezed orange juice

½ cup (120 mL) water, divided

1 medium-size jalapeno chili pepper, seeds removed and finely chopped, or use 1½ tsp (7 mL) chili powder

3 tbsp (45 mL) tamari

1 tbsp (15 mL) grated ginger root

1 large Vidalia onion, chopped

1 small parsnip, thinly sliced

1 medium carrot, grated

1 cup (250 mL) broccoli florets, cut into 1½-inch (4 cm) pieces

1 cup (250 mL) small frozen peas

1 tbsp (15 mL) cornstarch

1½ cups (350 mL) fresh or frozen mango, in 1-inch (2.5 cm) cubes

6 oz (170 g) whole grain rice vermicelli

3 tbsp (45 mL) fresh mint leaves, cut into strips

CHICKEN-SPINACH SLIDERS

MAKES 4 TO 6 SERVINGS

5 cups (1.2 L) spinach leaves, stems removed, rinsed, and chopped

1 shallot, finely diced

1 cup (250 mL) chopped chives, finely chopped

1 large garlic clove, finely chopped

1 tsp (5 mL) ground cumin

½ tsp (2 mL) sea salt

⅛ tsp (0.5 mL) black pepper

1 lb (454 g) ground chicken

¼ cup (60 mL) olive oil, divided

8 buns (toasted)

Sliced red onion, pickles, tomato slices, and mayonnaise for garnish

These little burgers pack a lot of flavor. You can use dinner rolls, pitas, or small slider buns. I have also used crumbled tempeh instead of ground chicken to make this recipe.

1. Combine the spinach, shallot, chives, garlic, cumin, salt, and pepper in a medium-size bowl. Add the chicken. Using a fork, mix gently, just to combine, and form the mixture into ten ½-inch (1 cm) thick patties.

2. Heat 2 tbsp (30 mL) oil in a large nonstick skillet over medium-high heat. Cook 5 patties at a time, about 5 minutes per side, until golden brown. Add the remaining oil to the pan and cook the remaining patties. Transfer to a plate and serve with buns and garnish.

SHAKSHUKA

MAKES 3 GENEROUS SERVINGS

I often do not have the time to skin and blanch ripe tomatoes. Instead, I buy good-quality cans of peeled whole tomatoes, usually Italian.

....

1. Heat the oil in a medium-size saucepan over medium heat. Add the shallots and garlic. Stir-fry the mixture for 5 minutes or until soft. Add the spices and cook for 2 more minutes, stirring.

2. Pour in the tomatoes, tomato paste, roasted red pepper, salt, and pepper. Break up the tomatoes, cover, and simmer for 10 minutes over low heat.

3. Make 6 spaces in the tomato sauce with the back of a large spoon. Break an egg into each space. Cover and cook for 5 minutes. Run a spoon through the yolks. Sprinkle with basil and serve.

3 tbsp (45 mL) olive oil

2 shallots, finely diced

3 garlic cloves, crushed

¾ tsp (4 mL) smoked paprika

½ tsp (2 mL) ground cumin

¼ tsp (1 mL) ground allspice

One 28-oz (796 mL) can plum tomatoes

2 tbsp (30 mL) tomato paste

½ cup (120 mL) chopped roasted red pepper

½ tsp (2 mL) sea salt

⅛ tsp (0.5 mL) black pepper

6 large eggs

½ cup (120 mL) fresh basil, chopped

GLOSSARY

Almond Butter
Pastes made from finely ground nuts or seeds are called "butters." Almond (smooth and crunchy), cashew, hazelnut, and sesame are used throughout this book. The fat in nuts and seeds is mono- and polyunsaturated. They contain no cholesterol but can be caloric and are best eaten in small amounts. Only buy nut and seed butters that do not have added sugar and refined oils.

Apple Cider Vinegar
Inexpensive, fruity tasting vinegar that needs refrigeration if unpasteurized. Its low level of acidity (4%) allows it to contribute flavor without overwhelming other ingredients, especially in salad dressing.

Aquafaba
The liquid that is found in a can of chickpeas. It is a very good binder straight from the can. It can be whipped and creates foam, which allows it to trap air, giving ingredients structure. I use it to replace egg whites in meringues!

Arugula
An important salad green ingredient, arugula is often added to the salad mix known as mesclun because of its peppery taste. It is related to the radish.

Balsamic Vinegar
Has a 6% level of acidity. Made from sweet Trebbiano grapes (skins and juice) that are crushed and fermented in wooden casks in the Italian region of Emilia-Romagna, near the town of Modena, Italy.

Balsamic is a Northern Italian vinegar made from white Trebbiano grape juice that becomes deep amber when aged in wood barrels. The mellow sweet-sour flavor best suits vinaigrette salad dressings or being splashed on steamed or grilled ingredients. Like most vinegars, it will keep indefinitely if stored in an airtight container. It need not be refrigerated. Expensive, especially if aged for 10 years or longer. But fortunately, a little goes a long way.

Balsamic Glaze
A glaze is thicker than a sauce, and something you can spread or "glaze" over ingredients.

Black Beans
Small, plump kidney-shaped beans with a shiny black-blue coat and an earthy flavor.

Brown Rice Vinegar
A mildly sweet vinegar made from fermented brown rice. Used extensively in Japanese and Chinese cuisines, rice vinegar enhances the flavor of plain rice. It is good in salad dressings and soy-based dips and sauces. It can be used as a pickling ingredient as well. Traditionally brewed, unfiltered rice vinegars often contain rice sediment that can make the liquid look cloudy. This is a sign of high quality.

Brown Sugar
Brown sugar is unrefined or partially refined sugar with some residual molasses content, or refined white sugar with molasses added. Available in light and dark varieties. The darker the color, the more intense the flavor.

Buckwheat
Has a strong, earthy flavor and is very porous, so it cooks quickly. Buckwheat groats are sold two ways, roasted or raw. They are one of the quickest cooking whole grains, taking only 15 minutes. Rinse raw buckwheat groats quickly, otherwise they absorb water and lose their shape. One way to keep the individual grains intact during cooking is to toast them first. I dry-roast buckwheat first to improve its texture, making it firmer and crunchier. When you combine an egg with the uncooked groats, the egg albumen helps the groats retain their shape. A gluten-free grain, buckwheat is related to rhubarb.

Canola Oil
Extracted from rapeseed, canola oil is clear, with little color. It is lower in saturated fat than any other oil and contains cholesterol-lowering omega-3 fatty acids. Use in baking and stir-frying.

Capers
Flower buds of a Mediterranean shrub that are pickled and used as a condiment.

cuisine camino

fair trade · équitable · BIOLOGIQUE

Bitters
chocolate
de choc

71% CACAO

Beurre d'am
biologiq

CRÈM

FAIR TRADE · ORGANIC ·

cuis
ca

camino
chocolate

cuisine
camino
fair trade · équitable

Vous trouverez de

cam

Cardamom

Grown in many parts of India, Mexico, and South America, cardamom is used in the sweet and savory dishes of many cuisines. Whole pods and ground cardamom are available. It has a complex, sweet-spicy flavor and aroma.

Cashew Butter

Pastes made from finely ground nuts are called "butters." They can be eaten out of the jar or used to cook in a recipe. Cashews are a fleshy tropical tree fruit that are enclosed in a tough shell. Their buttery, mellow flavor lends itself well to other dried and fresh fruits, coconut, and chocolate.

Chia

Seeds that are tiny ovals that can be black, white, or multihued. Black chia seeds come from the long-extended flowers of the chia plant. White chia seeds come from the small white flowers. They have a mild, nutty flavor. Chia seeds are high in protein and fiber.

Chickpeas

Small, round legumes with a tip and creamy beige color. Garbanzo is the Spanish name for chickpea. Available canned, frozen, or dried.

Chili Peppers

Chilies are available in many forms—fresh, dried, ground, or canned. The smaller the chili, the hotter it is. The heat is in the seeds and surrounding membrane. Their volatile oils can cause a lot of discomfort if you touch your mouth or eyes. You can protect yourself by wearing thin rubber gloves. Always wash your hands after handling. We use ancho, chipotle, jalapeno, and cayenne.

Cilantro

Herb with a distinct and hard-to-describe flavor that is quite polarizing. You either love it or you can't stand it! Cilantro is sometimes called coriander when you buy the fresh herb, but typically coriander refers to the dried seed or ground spice, and cilantro refers to the fresh leafy herbs. They are all part of the same plant.

Cocoa Powder

When combined with dark or bittersweet chocolate, cocoa powder adds a level of intensity to the flavor of a recipe. Cocoa beans are bitter and cannot be eaten raw. They are fermented, roasted, and aged. The roasted beans are then shelled and ground. In the process, the bean's natural fat, cocoa butter, is released. When this is removed, a dark chocolate paste known as cocoa liquor remains. It contains the flavor and aroma of chocolate. Cocoa powder is produced when the cocoa butter is removed from the cocoa liquor, leaving a dry cake that is ground into a fine powder.

Coconut Milk

Made by soaking shredded fresh coconut in hot water. When using canned coconut milk, make sure you mix the thin liquid at the top with the bottom creamy thick layer. Refrigerate leftover milk for a maximum of three days.

Coconut Oil

The coconut oil we tested our recipes with was from Maison Orphée–certified organic. It can be used as a healthy replacement for butter and margarine in recipes. When stir- and deep-frying, the ingredients do not absorb the oil. The pulp is grated, cold pressed, and filtered. There is no cholesterol in coconut oil, and it is not hydrogenated or deodorized. An excellent ingredient to introduce to a natural foods kitchen.

Cumin

Cumin seeds are the dried fruit of the cumin plant. Whole seeds and ground cumin are available in brown and black varieties. Cumin is often a part of another spice mixture, but can also be used on its own. Lightly toasting the seeds before grinding enhances their flavor.

Edamame

The name for the smooth green soybeans in the soybean pod. They are available fresh or frozen.

Fennel

Buy small bulbs that have the stalks and fuzzy fronds attached. You need to peel off the outer membrane and root end before using. Serve raw, thinly sliced, shaved, or braised in stock. Has a pronounced anise flavor and can be used interchangeably with celery.

MAISON ORPHÉE 🗝

FOR ENERGIZING COOKING
POUR UNE CUISINE ÉNERGISANTE

ORGANIC ❖ BIOLOGIQUE

Deodorized Coconut Oil
Huile de noix de coco désodorisée
454 g (16 oz)

Flax Seeds

Grinding flax seeds improves their digestibility. They make a good replacement for eggs in baking. One egg equals 1 tbsp (15 mL) ground flax seeds mixed with 3 tbsp (45 mL) liquid. Wait for 3 to 5 minutes and add to the wet ingredients. Ground flax seeds bind ingredients together. An excellent source of vitamin E and omega-3 fatty acids. Store ground flax seeds in the freezer.

Freekeh

An ancient grain that is a variety of wheat picked while still green. The outer husk is burnt off, leaving a chewy whole grain. It's a good source of protein and fiber that cooks in 15 to 20 minutes.

Garam Masala

The classic ground spice blend of Northern India. You can make it yourself or buy a ready-made spice blend. It contains cardamom seeds, cinnamon sticks, cumin seeds, whole cloves, black peppercorns, and nutmeg. I sprinkle it over roasting ingredients, stir-fries, or sautéed vegetables, rice, and nuts.

Greek Yogurt

Contains more protein than regular yogurt. The difference between Greek yogurt and regular yogurt is that they strain off the whey (watery part of the milk that remains) when the milk is curdled. The straining process makes the yogurt thick and creamy.

Hemp

Hempseed is a small, egg-shaped seed that forms in the tops of the plants. It is considered to be extremely nutritious and can be sprinkled over salad, used as a topping on granola, added to smoothies, or used as a garnish.

Kidney Beans

These versatile kidney-shaped beans can either be red or white. They tend to hold their shape during prolonged periods of cooking and so are often used in soups and stews.

Kombu

A sea vegetable often used as a soup and stock base. A strip of kombu cooked with water releases glutamic acid (a white powdery coating that contains a lot of flavor). Do not rinse it off before cooking. Glutamic acid is the natural version of the synthetic flavoring agent monosodium glutamate (MSG).

Lentils

A type of legume that is small and disc-shaped with a firm texture. Lentils do not need to be presoaked and, because they are flat with thin seed coats, they can easily be cooked. There are many kinds and colors of lentils—black, brown, green, orange, and red. I store my lentils in a glass jar, away from direct light.

Maple Syrup

A sweet syrup made from boiling the spring sap tapped from sugar maple trees. Graded according to color, flavor, and sugar content, maple syrups with a B or C designation can be used for baking and cooking. Grade A syrup is lighter, more delicate, and used as a topping for pancakes and ice cream.

Medjool Dates

They are large and plump, with a thick, moist flesh. They are delicious and expensive.

Mirin

A sweet rice wine used in Japanese cooking to balance the saltiness of other seasonings like miso and soy sauce. Can be used in sauces, glazes, and vinaigrettes. Mirin is made from water, sweet brown rice, and rice culture. It's a sweet, low-alcohol wine used for cooking. The alcohol evaporates upon contact with heat. Like sake, mirin is made from a mixture of rice koji (bacterial culture), cooked white rice, and water. It is thick, sweet, and pale golden. It balances the saltiness in miso and soy sauce.

Miso

Miso is to vegetarian cooking what beef bouillon or gravy is to a meat-centered diet. This salty, fermented paste is made from aged soybeans and usually grains. Thick and spreadable, it's used for flavoring a wide variety of recipes and as the basic ingredient in soup. It can also replace salt in recipes. Miso is available in several varieties in the refrigerated section of your local health food store. Dark miso tends to be saltier and have a stronger flavor than lighter varieties. Shiro, or white miso, has a pale yellow color and a mild taste. Miso will keep for six months when refrigerated in an airtight container.

Molasses

A strong-flavored, thick, dark liquid that remains after the sugar crystals have been removed from cane sugar. Used in baking. My favorite type is Barbados molasses, made from the first press of the sugar cane.

Nori

A sea vegetable with a briny flavor that has been dried and pressed into sheets. It's used for wrapping sushi rolls and also as a garnish when cut into thin strips or shredded. Sprinkle on corn on the cob and popcorn. It is also sold as flakes.

Oat Flour

Oat flour is finely milled oat groats. Oats are harvested with their hulls intact. Remove the hull and the remaining grain is the oat groat. If you cannot find oat flour, simply grind rolled oats (large flake) in a blender or spice grinder.

Oats: Steel Cut and Rolled

Steel Cut: Also called Irish oats. Made from oat groats that have been cut horizontally with a heavy steel blade. They require an overnight soaking or lengthy cooking.

Rolled: Available as large-flake rolled oats, quick-cooking rolled oats, and instant rolled oats.

Large-flake rolled oats are oat groats that have been heated to soften them, then rolled flat. Large-flake oats require 5 minutes of cooking. They are excellent for baking and have a coarse, chewy texture.

Quick-cooking rolled oats are rolled much thinner and require 1 to 2 minutes of cooking. Best used for cereal.

Instant rolled oats are steamed small flakes that are rolled and rehydrated in a hot liquid to use right away.

Olive Oil

Olive oil is pressed from olives. The first extraction is a simple pressing that does not heat the oil above room temperature and is filtered to remove pulp. The fruit has a fleshy pulp and the color ranges from black to mustard yellow and green. Virgin and extra virgin olive oil are recommended for cooking. Buy a good-quality olive oil packaged in dark-colored glass to protect it from sunlight. When olive oil is paired with tomatoes and garlic, it releases the flavor and health benefits of the other ingredients.

Pine Nuts

Seeds from the pinecones of evergreen trees. They are also called pignolias or piñons. Perishable and need to be refrigerated. Can be eaten raw or toasted.

Pinto Beans

Pinto beans are half the length of kidney beans and oval shaped. Their speckled coats range from brown to cranberry. A staple in Mexican cuisine, they are used in burritos, chili, and other refried bean dishes.

Quinoa

Quinoa is the size of a sesame seed. It is a nutritional powerhouse. Quinoa was one of the three staple foods, along with corn and potatoes, of the Inca civilization. Quinoa contains more protein than any other grain—an average of 16.2%. It grows in areas with high altitudes and low rainfall, and can grow in poor, sandy soil. Its adaptability has allowed it to grow in the high mountains of Ecuador, Peru, Bolivia, and southern Columbia, as well as Northern Argentina and Chile.

The grains are covered in saponin, an extremely bitter, resin-like substance. Quinoa must be rinsed in a fine mesh sieve under cold running water for 3 to 5 minutes or until the water runs clear. Bring water, stock, or juice to a boil before adding rinsed quinoa. Available as flour, pasta, and in flake form. Toast flour before using to remove saponin traces.

Rice Vermicelli

A dried noodle that comes in a variety of thicknesses. Available in whole wheat versions at supermarkets.

Rice Vinegar

Made from fermented rice. Light, honey-colored sweetish vinegar with a mild acidity level of 4%. Do not buy "seasoned" rice vinegar—the seasoning interferes with the natural flavors.

Sesame Seeds

These have a pleasant, nut-like flavor that can enhance any recipe. Often sold raw, they benefit from being toasted. Their delicious, nutty flavor combines so well with other nuts. Available as white and black, I recommend buying white sesame seeds at a health food store, where the seeds are sold unbleached and may be beige in color. Black sesame seeds are often more expensive and have the same flavor as white sesame seeds.

Soba Noodles

Long, thin Japanese noodles made from 100% buckwheat flour or a combination of buckwheat and unbleached or whole wheat flours. Soba comes in

Tempeh

several varieties with varying percentages of buckwheat. Other ingredients can be added for extra flavor. These noodles are eggless and less sticky than Italian pastas.

Soy Sauce and Tamari

Good-quality soy sauce is made from organic soybeans mixed with a bacterial culture and a grain—usually cracked roasted wheat. The mixture is fermented and salted and left to age for up to 2½ years, then strained and bottled. You can buy wheat-free soy sauce. Eden has an excellent brand. Salt-reduced soy sauce needs to be refrigerated after opening. The smaller the amount of salt used in making the soy sauce the shorter the shelf life. Tamari is a Japanese form of soy sauce that contains little or no wheat.

Spelt Flour

One of the ancient grains, spelt is a strain of wheat. It has a texture similar to standard wheat but with a different genetic profile. It can be substituted for whole wheat flour (soft or pastry).

Tahini

A thick, smooth paste made of hulled and ground sesame seeds. A Middle Eastern staple, tahini is used as a spread and as an ingredient in dressings, sauces, and dips.

Tempeh

A high-protein cultured food made from soybeans and grains. Invented in Indonesia, tempeh is traditionally made by culturing cooked, cracked soybeans with the mold Rhizopus oligosporus. The fermentation process enhances the flavor, and the enzymes from the mold break down the complex proteins, fats, and carbohydrates of the soybean, making them easier to digest. Tempeh has a firm, chewy texture and a mild mushroom taste. Tempeh can be steamed, fried, deep-fried, braised, crumbled, microwaved, or poached. Sold fresh (check expiry date) and frozen (keeps six months in the freezer), tempeh will thaw overnight in the refrigerator or three hours on your countertop.

Toasted Sesame Oil

Made from toasted sesame seeds. Darker in color than plain sesame oil, with a wonderful aroma. Not to be confused with sesame oil, which has a milder, less-distinct flavor. They are not interchangeable.

Tofu

Sometimes called bean curd, tofu is a white, neutral-tasting, easily digestible soy food. To make tofu, soybeans are soaked, drained, and ground. The ground beans are simmered in water, strained, and pressed to produce soy milk. A coagulant is then added to the soy milk, which causes curds to form. The curds are placed in perforated boxes and the amount of weight that is placed on top of the boxes is determined by the required firmness of the tofu. Extra firm, firm, and medium firm all reflect the amount of water allowed to remain.

Prepackaged tofu should always be rinsed before use. Once opened, the unused portion of tofu can be refrigerated, submerged in water, for five days. To ensure freshness, change the water every second day. Leftover tofu can be frozen for a maximum of six months. It must be defrosted before using.

Turmeric

Fresh turmeric looks like a dark piece of ginger with thin stalks. It is bright orange and difficult to grind. It is often used in spice blends. Use it sparingly—too much turmeric tastes bitter. Used in dal and curries.

Wasabi Powder

Wasabi is a light green Japanese root vegetable that is very hot, with a taste reminiscent of horseradish. It is sold dried and powdered. For cooking or serving as a condiment, the powder is mixed with water and made into a paste.

Whole Wheat Flour (Soft or Pastry)

Finely ground, it is made from softer wheat that is lower in protein but contains some of the bran and germ. It is used for cakes and pastries.

Wine Vinegars

Stronger than grain-based vinegars, with a 6% to 7% level of acidity. The deeper the color, the stronger the flavor, and the more pronounced the taste and ability of the vinegar to flavor the food or dressing. Wine vinegars are made from red or white wines and range from mild to strong in taste, often depending on the type of wine and the length of fermentation.

ACKNOWLEDGMENTS

What Was Used:

Cha's Organics provided four kinds of excellent-quality Fairtrade organic coconut milk, Fairtrade organic spices, and teas. Marise May and Chanaka Kurera work with Sri Lankan farmers.
www.chasorganics.com

Cuisinart provided the Cuisinart Elite Collection 12-Cup Food Processor that was used for recipe testing in the book. This indispensable kitchen appliance came in handy for the dips, main courses, and desserts.
www.cuisinart.ca

Equifruit provided Fairtrade bananas. Thanks to Kim Chackal and Jenny Coleman. It is so wonderful to see Fairtrade bananas in supermarkets and health food stores.
www.equifruit.com

La Siembra Co-operative, distributor of Camino Fairtrade and organic products from a Canadian worker co-op based in Ottawa, Ontario, supplied me with the highest-quality cocoa powders, chocolate and chocolate chips, coconut, and four types of sugar. Thanks to Melanie Broguet and Tom Hanlon-Wilde.
info@camino.ca

Merchants of Green Coffee provided coffee beans. Thanks to Meagan Thibeault and Derek Zavislake, located at 2 Matilda Street, Toronto, Ontario.
www.merchantsofgreencoffee.com

Maison Orphée supplied me with the highest-quality coconut and toasted sesame oil, mustard, vinegars, and sea salt. Thanks to Charlotte Lemaire.
info@maisonorphee.com

Nuts to You donated products from their line of almond, cashew, peanut, pumpkin, and tahini butters. Thanks to Sam Abrams, Anna Janes, and Anne Lawrence.
www.nutstoyounutsbutter.com

The Palestine Fair Trade Association provided me with olive oil, za'atar, and freekeh. Their bottles of Nabali and Rumi olive oil were used to test the recipes in this book. Many thanks to Fida Abdallah. Their olive oil can be shipped to Canada.
www.canaanpalestine.com

Traditional Medicinals provided me with a terrific assortment of fair trade organic teas that were used to cook with and drink while making this book. Thanks to Brian White.
www.ca.traditionalmedicinals.com

Zwilling J. A. Henckels provided my knives and other kitchen tools. Their bamboo cutting boards, stainless steel whisks, pots, and pans were useful for properly testing recipes.
www.zwilling.ca

The Best Recipe Testers in the World:

Leonie Eidinger	Raquel Fox	Reggie Levack
Debra Fingold	Heather Howe	Ken Thompson
Adrienne Forbes	Umay Kurmoo	

Photography Team:

Mike McColl. What a genius. You listened and turned the recipes into works of rustic art. Your creativity and attention to detail were outstanding. Thanks to Lucia McColl for her assistance as well.

Gina St. Germain, Food and Prop Stylist. I would find Gina standing on a chair, diving into my top shelf, back of the cupboard, looking for that perfect plate to match a recipe. This is on top of the 100 other plates she had brought. Creative, innovative, and so stylish.

Heather Howe, PHEc, lead recipe tester. Heather is a treasure trove of culinary information. Such a pleasure to work with and learn from. Visit www.livintocook.ca.

Mackenzie Bird, computer assistant extraordinaire.

Éric St. Pierre, Fairtrade ingredient photos.

For Editorial Guidance and Support:

Jocie Bussin	Mary Sharpe	JD Singh
Marian Masters	Suzie Siegal	Dorice Tepley

The Team at Whitecap:

Andrew Bagatella   Sharon Fitzhenry   Patrick Geraghty
Holly Doll

To My Fair Trade Board Friends and Colleagues:

Thank you for your time, expertise, and effort in promoting fair trade practices and policies in Canada and internationally.

Lloyd Bernhardt   John Kay   Adam Tampuri
Harry Cook   Marise May   Hugues Tshibemba
Eric Crowell   Nick Orton   Stephanie Wells
Naji Harb   Janet Riehm

My Family:

Husband Jim Urquhart. Children Cameron, Mackenzie, and Emery. Thank you for your support and patience.

INDEX